BREEDING
ANGELFISH
FOR THE HOBBYIST & PROFESSIONAL

Pet Reference Series No. 2

STEVEN DOW

The Palmetto Publishing Company
4747 - 28th Street North • St. Petersburg, Florida
(813) 522-3453
33714

© 1976 Steven Dow
Palmetto Publishing Co.
St. Petersburg, Florida

All rights reserved. No part of this book may be reproduced in any manner without the prior written permission of the publisher.

Library of Congress Cataloging in Publication Data

Dow, Steven.
    Breeding angelfish for the hobbyist & professional.

    (Pet reference series; no. 2)
    Includes index.
    1. Angel fish—Breeding. 2. Angel fish. I. Title.
SF458.A5D68   639'.375'8   76-1982
ISBN 0-915096-04-8

This book has been set in Palatino 10 point by Photocomp, Inc., using a computerized process and printed in America by the Great Outdoors Press, St. Petersburg, Florida

CONTENTS

1. IDENTIFICATION OF ANGELFISH — 1
2. THE VARIETIES OF ANGELFISH — 6
3. CARE AND MAINTENANCE — 11
4. NUTRITION — 15
5. DISEASES — 19
6. BEGINNING TO BREED ANGELFISH — 25
7. THE SPAWNING — 30
8. ALLOWING PARENTAL CARE — 34
9. THE DEVELOPING SPAWN — 40
10. SMALL SCALE BREEDING OF ANGELFISH — 53
11. INSTALLATION OF A HATCHERY ROOM — 58
12. SELLING THE BABY ANGELFISH — 67

APPENDIX A: SELECTIVE BREEDING OF ANGELFISH — 75
APPENDIX B: DEVELOPING AN EXPERIMENTAL ATTITUDE — 80
APPENDIX C: SEXING ANGELFISH — 83
COLOR PLATES — 85
INDEX — 93

ACKNOWLEDGEMENT

I would like to take this opportunity to thank those who assisted me in bringing this book into being. Thanks are due to Mr. Fred Rackmil, editor of Pet Dealer magazine, who was the inspiration helping to materialize the idea of this book. Secondly, I would like to thank Mr. Fred Cochu, president of Paramount Aquarium, Inc. and his wife, Dorothy, for their invaluable technical assistance and advice in my earlier years of studying angelfish. Their years and years of experience proved vital in formulating some of the theories set forth in this book. Gratitude is also due to Mr. Robert Rodriguez, MBA, for his assistance in the organization of the material. Finally, I would like to acknowledge deep gratitude to my wife, Daniele, who inspired my thoughts and aided me enormously during my many evenings at the typewriter.

> G. Steven Dow
> Orlando, Fla.

FOREWARD

Steven Dow is no newcomer to the tropical fish scene. He has spent many years actively engaged in one aspect or another of the hobby. But whatever else claimed his attention, he always found time to pursue his love of breeding fish. Having specialized with angelfish, he is now able to produce these fish in quantity without any undue complications.

The techniques he uses are mainly of his own devising, perfected after many trials and tribulations.

During his early endeavors to breed angels, he found it difficult to find helpful published literature on the subject. Now that he has accomplished the desired results by personal experimentation, he decided to write this book so that his fellow aquarist could be provided with the information he sought unsuccessfully in his early days.

Steven Dow's background and practical experience with tropical fish qualifies him admirably for preparing this book. He has been a practicing aquarist since childhood, and a professional breeder and dealer in adult life. In mastering the art of breeding angelfish, he acquired knowledge of the type of information that should be included in a comprehensive work.

Although Steven Dow has devoted this book exclusively to the breeding and rearing of angelfish, either for fun or profit, much of the information could be applied equally well to other species of Cichlid.

The very readable text, supported by appropriate illustrations will be appreciated by all who wish to breed angelfish. It will be of special interest to those hobbyists who have tried and failed, and those who wish to tread the path for the first time.

Robert F. O'Connell.

To Daniele, my loving wife and inspiration

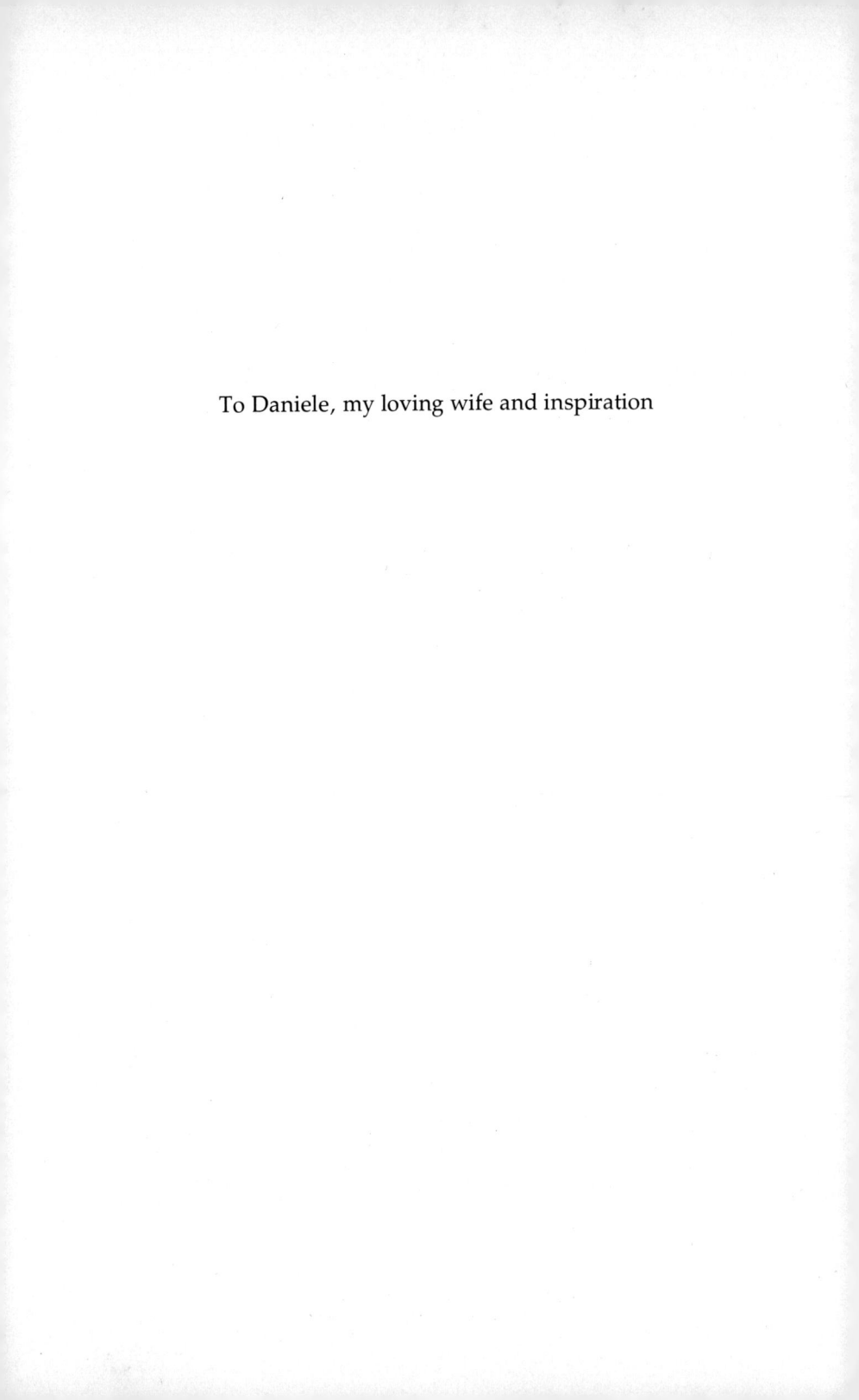

1. IDENTIFICATION OF ANGELFISH

Pterophyllum scalare, (pronounced: TAIR'-o-Fill'-lum ska-LAIR'-e)

Meaning of name: ptero: wing, or winged, phyllum: leaf, or leaf-like, scalare: reminiscent of a stairway, ladder-like

Natural Distribution: Amazon River, Rio Negro, Orinoco River & parts of Guiana

TYPE OF HABITAT Angelfish reportedly breed naturally in flooded reed beds in mid-January. It is interesting to note how well their natural coloration and body formation equip them for survival in such areas. One can readily imagine them gliding effortlessly through reed-choked passages. In the shadowy light they are nearly invisible, their vertical black stripes blending with the quivering shadows of the reeds. Like living phantoms, they weave gracefully through the inundated undergrowth, feeding freely upon the abundant supply of newly born aquatic insects, crustaceans, and small fishes. Imagine a pair busily preparing a spawning site upon a sturdy green reed, valiantly defending the site against all intruders. Such are some of the natural spawning conditions of angelfish.

At other times, they inhabit rocky banks and dwell among fallen logs and branches, living mostly in slow-moving or still waters. Angelfish prefer areas which afford adequate hiding places and allow convenient retreat from dangerous predators.

CLASSIFICATION Angelfish are classified as Cichlids, sharing their family with some of the most intelligent of tropical fishes. The fin structure of angelfish, which contains both hard and soft rays, is a typical feature of the Cichlids. Their breeding behavior, care of fry, and shape of the young are characteristics shared by most Cichlids. The Cichlid family is among the more highly evolved of the fresh-water fishes.

SUBPHYLUM:	CRANIATA
CLASS:	OSTEICHTHYES
SUBCLASS:	ACTINOPTERYGII
SUPERORDER:	TELEOSTEI
ORDER:	PERCIFORMES
SUBORDER:	PEROCOIDEI
FAMILY:	CICHLIDAE
GENUS:	*PTEROPHYLLUM*
SPECIES:	*scalare*
	eimekei
	altum
	dumerilii

BODY FORM AND COLORATION Angelfish possess the universally recognized elongated dorsal and anal fins which give rise to the "ptero" of their generic name. The ventral fins also are modified in angelfish, descending as long trailing feelers. These feelers do not move freely, as with anabantids, but apparently are used as sensors, perhaps for sensing vibrations or locating obstructions to passage, not unlike a cat's whiskers.

Angelfish possess, in nature, four body stripes upon a silvery field. The first stripe transverses and camouflages the eye. The second stripe emanates from the forward base of the dorsal fin vertically down the body to the anal fin. The third stripe passes from the tip of the dorsal fin through the body to the hind base of the anal fin, continuing through the anal fin itself. The final stripe is situated on the caudal peduncle. In healthy unmutated natural stock additional physical characteristics found are as follows: black pimplelike spots on the upper sides of the body, a sheen of iridescent blue appears on the lower body near the gill covers, a brownish gold sheen at the crown — especially in adult fish in breeding condition, and reddish-orange eyes when the fish are in excellent health.

These attractive factors contribute to the delightful appearance of angelfish. Unique in stately ornamental beauty, they possess a quality equalled by few tropical fishes.

TEMPERATURE REQUIREMENTS Ideal aquarium temperature for angelfish is usually given between 68 and 90 degrees F. (20 to 32 degrees. C.) While the maintenance of this temperature range is usually critical, inadvertently some of the author's angelfish were subjected to overnight temperatures as low as 50 degrees F. and they survived. This happened to mated pairs kept in an unheated garage, and was the result of an unanticipated early frost. Angelfish will not feed at these low temperatures because of their lowered metabolic rate, but they can survive at these low temperatures for several hours without ill effects, providing the temperature change is gradual. When returned to normal temperatures, the author's breeders were spawning regularly again within three weeks. Some fry subjected to this low temperature were lost, but most survived.

Angelfish can live, for short periods, in temperatures above 90 degrees F. as well. Having had heaters malfunction with resulting temperatures rising above 95 degrees F. for several hours, the author can report that angelfish endure this heat, provided the water is well aerated. In similarly recorded instances when aquarium water rose above 90 degrees F. and the fish survived, the water was always well oxygenated. Were this not the case, temperatures above 90 degrees F. would rapidly become fatal due to oxygen deficiency resulting in suffocation.

While mentioning known instances where angelfish tolerated extremes of temperature other than those limits given in standard aquarium literature, it is evident that temperatures either above or below the standard tolerances are fatal or seriously debilitating if endured over extended periods.

From 72 degrees to 85 degrees F. should be considered the proper maintenance range, whereas 50 degrees to 100 degrees F. is the survival range. Beyond these extremes, death occurs rapidly.

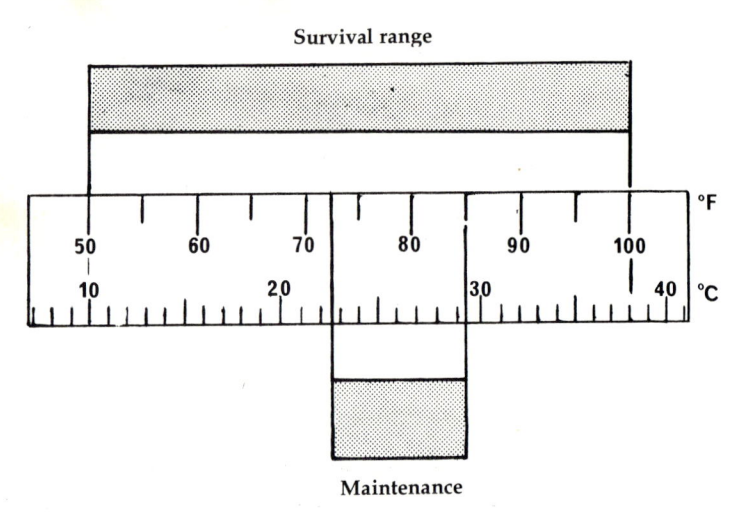

Fig. 1. Scale showing temperature tolerance and ideal range.

FOUR TYPES OF ANGELFISH Four genera of angelfish (*Pterophyllum*) have been identified by ichthyologists to date. They are: *P. scalare, P. eimekei, P. altum,* and *P. dumerilii*. *P. scalare* was previously described as *Zeus scalaris,* an inspired name granting royal status to a regal fish. Angelfish have been reclassified numerous times since then, but the present name *P. scalare* will probably remain valid.

Apparently *P. scalare* and *P. eimekei* are one and the same fish, or tank-raised specimens are a hybrid of the two. This question has never been satisfactorily resolved, although most authorities do now consider these to be the same species. It is quite probable that they are one species merely taken from different geographical areas.

P. altum is so much like *P. scalare* that it takes a practiced eye to distinguish the minute differences. *P. altum* are rare in captivity, although they are commercially available from time to time as both wild adults and tank-raised juveniles. They are slightly larger than *P. scalare* as well as being slightly more compressed from head to tail. Aside from these slight differences, *P. altum* are practically indistinguishable from *P. scalare*.

This is not the case with *P. dumerilii*, which is easily distinguishable, even to an inexperienced eye. The stripes on *P. dumerilii* are less distinct, and judging from available photographs, they have a somewhat hawkish appearance, as opposed to *P. altum* which strikes one as being almost canarylike. *P. scalare* possesses the least protruding mouth structure of the three varieties.

At the present time *P. altum* must be considered as a scarce fish, and *P. dumerilii* as a rarity. While these two known species are mentioned here in passing, this book will deal exclusively with *Pterophyllum scalare*, since this is the angelfish that most aquarists are likely to encounter. Breeding is certainly nearly identical for all species of *Pterophyllum*.

HISTORICAL BRIEF The first published reports concerning the breeding of angelfish in captivity date as early as 1917 by Rauschenberg. Little is known of the commercial value of these early spawnings, but we can suspect the thrill, excitement, and frustration that must have accompanied such an event. Imagine being presented with a spawn of some 500 young angelfish worth a virtual fortune, and yet being unable to dispose of them for lack of an established market. What a frustrating experience it must have been!

Large scale commercial breeding of angelfish began late in the 1930's, after a tropical fish market had already been carefully established. Following World War II, angelfish were bred in enormous quantities throughout America and the rest of the world, until today angelfish are a common sight anywhere in the civilized world where aquarium fish are sold.

THE FOUR TYPES OF ANGELFISH

Pterophyllum scalare	(Lichenstein)	1823
Pterophyllum eimekei	(Ahl)	1828
Pterophyllum altum	(Pellegrin)	1903
Pterophyllum dumerilii	(Castelnau)	1855

2. THE VARIETIES OF ANGELFISH

There are at least sixteen separate varieties of *Pterophyllum scalare* being marketed commercially today. Over the next ten years, we are likely to see at least another 10 varieties arrive upon the retail marketplace. Angelfish with extra fins have already been reported on several occasions. Angelfish have been produced with two dorsal fins and two anal fins. Imagine the possibilities of a blue, brown, red, or green angelfish with a double dorsal, double anal, multi-tailed combination. Such a bizarre fish, if properly developed, would rival the marine turkeyfish in bizarre appearance. It is only a matter of time until these fish are eventually offered for sale in retail shops. The possible combinations are almost endless.

The various angelfish types that have been successfully bred and marketed are listed below. Each color variety in the following listing can occur in the veiltail form as well as in the normal finned form. These mutant combinations will not be listed separately.

TYPES OF ANGELFISH

SILVER ANGELFISH This is the naturally occurring variety of angelfish with four vertical black stripes on a silver background. A sheen of turquoise and gold are usually present on healthy adult specimens. The eyes of all angelfish exhibit a fiery red-orange hue when the fish are in top condition.

SILVER VEILTAIL This strain is a fin mutant rather than a color variety. The fins of silver veiltailed angelfish are long, lacy, and gracefully flowing. There are apparently two distinct genetic conditions: those angelfish with long veiltails and those with extra long veiltails. While the extra long finned fish are exquisitely beautiful and make delightful show fish, they should not be used for breeding.

Any veiltailed strain of fish intended for breeding, no matter what the color variety, should be chosen from among those fish having medium fin development. This simplifies care of the breeders, which are less prone to disease if shorter finned, and the fry are universally more robust and disease resistant themselves.

BLACK LACE ANGELFISH This variety is lacy black, but has visible black stripes. These fish make striking display specimens, expecially the veiltail variety. When a pair of black lace spawn, count on about 20% being valuable pure black angelfish. It is wise to isolate black babies from their more robust black lace brothers and sisters. Breeding black lace to black will produce a large percentage of black offspring that are hardier than those produced by black to black crosses.

BLACK ANGELFISH Strikingly beautiful, both normal blacks and veiltail blacks are in great demand. The supply of black and black veiled angelfish has never approached the national demand and probably never will. A shrewd, industrious breeder of black and black veiled angelfish in a large metropolitan area could quickly build a thriving enterprise by producing these fish in quantity. Although much work is involved in raising high quality black and black veiled angelfish, the extra work is justified due to the higher price commanded by these beautiful fish.

MARBLE ANGELFISH A relative newcomer, but a completely established variety on the market, this strain is extremely hardy. Considering that each fish is different provides explosive grounds for experimentation with possible mutations as a goal. One could conceivably produce fish with black faces and white bodies, or fish with a white spot on the side of an otherwise black body. A couple of years of dedicated careful inbreeding is probably all that is necessary.

BLUSH ANGELFISH Blushing angelfish were developed in Connecticut, and are an attractive addition to the angelfish color varieties. The fish is pale white-silver with a blushing face. This appears so because the skin covering the gills is transparent and this exposes the red gill membrane. In typical spawns, some fry will be very blushed, some moderately so, and some not at all. This is normal. As the blushing angelfish matures, the blush on the face usually fades because the skin thickens in the adult fish. However, they will still produce excellent blushing offspring. A steady seller, the blush angelfish are sometimes in short supply at retail outlets.

GHOST ANGELFISH   This is nothing more than a blush angelfish without the blush. Although blushless ghost angelfish might sell well at Halloween, they are not to be recommended as a steady selling fish. Any large spawn of blush angelfish will yield at least 20% as ghost angelfish.

BLACKFINNED BLUSHING ANGELFISH Some strains of blush angels are being bred with black fins. This strain calls to mind an image of a Siamese cat, and is very popular among hobbyists. If this strain were unavailable locally, it could most likely be produced by starting with a cross between black lace and blush parents and selecting suitable breeding stock from the offspring.

GOLD ANGELFISH When these hit the national market around 1971, there was a noticeable gold rush. They commanded high prices, were sold quickly, and the first breeders presumably made substantial profits from their efforts. There was a mad scramble to get in on the initial windfall profits, but unfortunately, it was fools' gold!

Up to the age of roughly six months, when the golden hue appears, the young are primarily silver, resembling ordinary silver angelfish. Golden angelfish do not breed 100% true and there is no way of knowing which fish will turn gold and which will not.

In the six months waiting period to separate those angels which do turn gold, the total production of one breeder pair amounts to an inventory of over 5,000 large fish, requiring astronomical tank space and care. This is one strain of angelfish which is better left to the large Florida fish farms where they can be raised in dirt pools.

All that glitters is not golden angelfish.

HARLEQUIN ANGELFISH This strain is apparently not yet fixed, but is a normal stage of development in the transformation period of gold angels. Gold angelfish will first turn black, then gradually change to gold. During the month-long transformation, the fish are a beautiful gold and black marbleized pattern. This color stage is far prettier than the end result, the golden angelfish. It is a shame that these were not developed instead of the washed-out golden angels since they would be a phenomenal success.

ZEBRA ANGLEFISH Another recent strain which has been marketed successfully is the zebra angelfish, a carefully developed inbred cross between black lace and marble angelfish. Each specimen is slightly different, not unlike the marble angelfish to which they are closely related. This strain is rapidly gaining in popularity despite its present high price. The zebra angel is a hardy fish that the amateur breeder can satisfactorily reproduce and which has a ready market.

HALF-BLACK ANGELFISH Not exceptionally popular, there is still a slight demand for this strain. The rear half of the body is black, the front is silver. While the fish is not breathtaking, it displays a certain beauty. With demand remaining slight, the price is fairly high, probably because few breeders bother with them.

A bit of mystery surrounds this strain. It is claimed to be foundation stock for the present black angelfish in America by some European breeders. The half-black strain apparently did originate in Europe, if available information is to be believed. American breeders, if any really know the answer, remain silent on the subject. It seems plausible that the half-blacks could be the foundation stock for black and black lace angelfish, but it will probably never be proven. One fact that tends to discredit the theory that blacks come from half-blacks is that in many years of breeding black lace angelfish the author never encountered a single throwback half-black.

SMOKY ANGELFISH At times these are sold in fish stores. They have been included here, although they are not bred commercially due to the low public demand. Smoky angelfish resemble a poor quality marble angelfish and give an impression of being out of focus.

RED, BROWN, ALBINO, BLUE, AND GREEN ANGELFISH From time to time rumors spread that someone is secretly developing a strain of either blue, red, brown, green, albino, or some other new variety of angelfish. More often than not, this is wishful thinking. At the time of this writing, summer of 1975, none of the above are commercially available, with the exception of greens being offered by a hatchery in Hong Kong. When these strains finally appear on the market, they are bound to create an immediate sensation. Whoever first develops these strains will be able to quickly sell all that can be produced at a sizable profit.

Albino angelfish have frequently been reported, but to date all have been exceedingly weak specimens. Eventually, a strong albino will arrive in some lucky breeder's tanks, and this strain will be fixed.

STRAIN CROSSES With several color varieties of angelfish existing, all the same species, occasionally an imaginative entrepreneur will cross blush angelfish with black lace and start an apparently new strain. Zebra blushes and half-black blushes are other possibilities. While these fish are unusual, they can be produced by anyone whenever desired.

MULTIPLE FINNED ANGELFISH While multifinned angelfish may not be developed commercially during our lifetimes, it is merely a matter of time until there are veiltailed angelfish with two or even three tails, a couple of dorsal fins, and perhaps a couple of anal fins as well. It is a matter of speculation whether such grotesque mutations would become popular, but considering the intense interest lavished upon marine Lion Fish (*P. volitans*), when they finally do appear, they are certain to create an aquatic sensation.

3. CARE AND MAINTENANCE

Basic care of angelfish can be divided into three fundamental areas: nutrition, stability of environment, and cleanliness. Of these, nutrition will be dealt with in a later chapter. The remaining two factors, stability of environment and cleanliness, will be discussed in this chapter.

Considering the environmental stability first, we must realize that in the area where angelfish are found in nature, the Amazon rain forest rivers and streams of Brazil, we find an unusually stable environment. Situated in the equatorial tropics, the temperature of the rivers and their tributaries is extremely stable. Water temperatures rise and fall very slowly, while the range of temperature fluctuations is also quite narrow, varying no more than a couple of degrees in any given month.

As a point of reference, assume that the water temperature fluctuates less than one degree in any 24 hour period. In such a stable environment, the angelfish remains strong and healthy to fight the natural hazards of his wild existence.

Transposing this angelfish to the home aquarium and placing him in an artificial environment such as a 10 gallon cubical, his resistance will naturally be considerably lowered. Adding to these unfamiliar (to the angelfish) conditions, a daily temperature shift of ten to fifteen degrees F. in the aquarium is one reason why so many people meet with failure when attempting to maintain and breed angelfish.

The remarkable fact that angelfish can survive and even

thrive under our unwitting abuses certainly vouches for the hardiness of the species.

As potential fish breeders, a rational consideration of the probable long range effects of temperature instability is beneficial. Even though some angelfish strains are less vulnerable than others, careful maintenance of a satisfactory temperature with minimal fluctuation contributes to obtaining the most desirable results.

The best way to maintain a constant aquarium temperature is to keep a controlled room temperature. Thermostatically controlled heating and air conditioning, whenever possible, are ideal for a fish room or small hatchery.

Obviously, for many aquarists, a centrally heated fish room is out of the question. In such cases, if adequate insulation is installed, and temperature extremes can be prevented in the fish room, moderately priced aquarium heaters provide an excellent means of maintaining temperature stability.

Heaters may be installed and set slightly below the daily average temperature. They will then remain inactive unless the aquarium temperature falls below the preset position.

Water chemistry also figures prominently as a stability factor. Constantly tampering with the pH and/or hardness is both senseless and destructive. Environmental stability is of primary importance. Imperfect stable conditions are preferable to those where the novice aquarist constantly risks the health of his fish with needless alterations.

The best method of maintaining water chemistry stability consists of frequent partial water changes and weekly siphoning of accumulated debris in the breeding aquariums. The water changes help to maintain pH and hardness stability by dilution of dissolved minerals and wastes which could otherwise alter the pH and hardness.

Lighting, also, must be stable and predictable to ensure success with angelfish breeders. Few hobbyists would suddenly light a darkened aquarium at night without first allowing for a gradual increase in the room lighting. Some hobbyists do unwittingly fail to follow a proper pattern in their lighting, however.

This type of environmental instability leads to fright and disorientation.

For this reason, it is wise to install a timer on the lighting system. A good timer, like an electric memory, will maintain a definite routine which is reassuring to breeding anglefish.

Fish room activity should likewise be as routine as possible. While most angelfish today are less skittish than their wild counterparts, they nevertheless are more at ease when fish room movements follow a definite pattern.

Even though there is an ever-present temptation to proudly show off the fish room to friends, the gestures of unfamiliar people often disturb mature anglefish. If guests are unavoidable, allow them only at a set period, preferably after the fish have eaten a heavy afternoon meal and are less excitable.

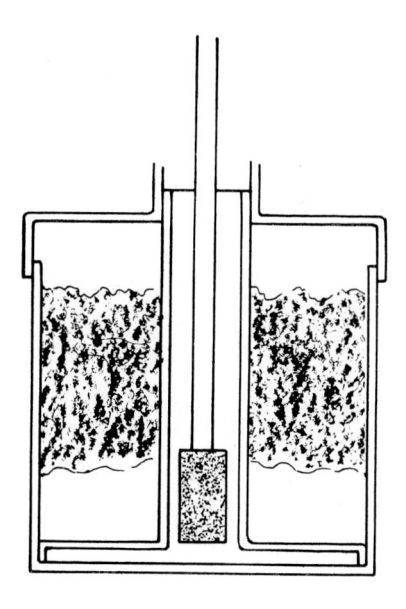

Fig. 2. Corner filter showing how filter media is packed between two layers of filter floss.

Aquarium cleanliness is another major consideration of the serious aquarist and advanced hobbyist. Realizing the importance of prevention, the successful aquarist avoids dirty and crowded conditions which can kill his fish. The excessive build-up of fish wastes in the aquarium can inhibit growth, stop mating activity, and lead to premature deaths of adult angelfish. Cleanliness means regular cleaning of filters and routine siphoning of aquariums, and is a key requisite to success in breeding angelfish.

Filter cleaning need not follow an inflexible schedule, but it is always best to clean a number of the filters daily to prevent accumulating too many at one time.

Cleanliness is also maintained by careful feeding practices. Overfeeding must be avoided and uneaten food netted out daily to prevent harmful bacterial growths from developing.

The size of an aquarium which houses a mated pair usually determines the frequency of periodic maintenance; but a pair housed in a well maintained and spotlessly clean 10 gallon aquarium is certainly better off than a pair maintained in an unkept and unclean twenty gallon aquarium.

If environmental stability and cleanliness are consistently practiced, along with sound nutritional habits outlined in the following chapter, success with angelfish is virtually insured.

4. NUTRITION

The correct diet for tropical fishes is important to health, and can prevent many diseases, provided a little thought is given to variety and nutritious substances. Scientists are only beginning to understand the important role nutrition plays in the prevention of diseases in both man and other animals. There is every reason for assuming that nutritional knowledge applies to captive tropical aquarium fishes as well.

It is common practice for tropical fish enthusiasts to stress the importance of live foods in the diets of tropical fish. Less often is it explained why such diets and feedings are important. Just as adequate levels of vitamin C in the systems of humans prevents scurvy, fresh and live foods containing unadulterated vitamins, minerals, and perhaps other as yet unidentified substances, are highly beneficial to the health of tropical fishes maintained in captivity. All other factors being equal, it is certain that fish fed live foods live longer than fish fed entirely upon prepared dried foods.

It cannot be stressed enough that breeding fishes should be fed some sort of live food at least once a week. This will not only increase the productive lifespan of breeding angelfish, but will increase the fertility of males and the egg production of females as well. It is known that a lack of vitamin E in rats inhibits reproduction entirely. There are certainly equally important minerals and vitamins essential to the reproductive activities of tropical fishes as well.

While nobody knows the result of vitamin deficiencies in fishes, it is certain that such deficiencies would lower disease resistance. Careful feeding of vitamin-rich foods will ensure the highest degree of health for angelfish as well as all other tropical aquarium fishes. Freshness of foods applies doubly when breeding is desired.

Some of the easily obtainable live foods are: daphnia, earthworms, mosquito larva, fruit flies, cyclops, and baby fishes. Small amounts of such foods given at least once a week will significantly contribute to breeding success with angelfish.

Frozen foods are nearly as nutritious, but some vitamin potency and nutritional value are undoubtedly lost in the freezing process. Beef-heart and brine shrimp are excellent frozen foods and are readily available in most areas. Other forms of frozen foods are satisfactory; such tasty morsels as lobster, shrimp, squid, clams, oysters, scallops, fish, or lean beef are excellent and readily accepted by the fish. Freshness (of the food) is most important in determining the maximum available benefit from the food.

Dry foods provide tropical fish with some necessary roughage which aids in preventing constipation. A steady diet of only dry foods, however, will seriously reduce angelfish breeding activities. Angelfish spawn at 6 to 8 week intervals when fed an exclusive diet of dry foods, whereas they may be induced to spawn as frequently as every seven days when the diet includes fresh foods and some live foods.

Dry foods shelved over six months are less nourishing than when freshly packed. Cooking, drying, and preparing these foods robs fish of valuable trace elements and vitamins, but when sitting on a dealer's shelf or at home for long periods, these foods lose the few remaining vitamins still present after processing.

All fish foods should be kept cool and away from humidity. Only such quantities as the fish will normally consume within two months should be purchased at one time. It is essential to carefully choose a reliable source of dry fish food where freshness is assured.

Frequent small feedings daily are better than two or three

large meals. This is no surprise to tropical fish fanciers or fish breeders. Almost every tropical fish book written recommends frequent light feedings, rather than one or two big daily feedings for breeding angelfish (or any other fish).

This is because it was long ago discovered that heavy meals taken infrequently cause extensive abdominal pressures and severely tax the digestive system of fishes. What wisdom could a fish fancier have in forcing his fish to gorge themselves at one large meal daily, then suffer throughout the remainder of the day, being forced to absorb their body tissues for nourishment? Such feeding practices markedly shorten the lives of producing breeders and reduce the numbers of fry one may expect a mated pair to produce.

Two factors generally considered important in angelfish nutrition are: frequency of feeding and freshness of foods. While these factors are little emphasized elsewhere and research is inconclusive, common sense suggests the wisdom of these two guides. Remembering that in natural circumstances fish feed continuously throughout the daylight period, mostly on natural live foods, it must be concluded that their systems have evolved dependent upon constant feeding. By attempting to duplicate these conditions in the aquariums as nearly as possible, healthier, longer living fishes will be the certain result.

Like spoiled children, angelfish continually fed the same unvaried diet will eat nothing else. Little can be done for such fish; one can only continue the unbalanced diet. They may prefer to starve rather than willingly eat something besides that which they are accustomed to eating.

If one begins with young fish, it is best to train them to eat a wide variety of foods, varying the protein source daily. A suitable dry food is given at least once daily. For subsequent meals, a variety of protein rich foods should always be given.

Two separate protein foods should be fed twice daily. Choosing from the accompanying list of fresh and live foods, a dietary schedule can be quickly devised to accommodate the growing fishes without incurring too much expense. Often fresh foods are less expensive than the dry foods!

Freeze-dried foods are beneficial to breeders and young fish alike. Freeze-dried brine shrimp, tubifex worms, and beef hearts are excellent. Other such foods continue to appear on the market as time passes; such foods as mosquito larva, crickets, clams, and squid are among those that are often offered for purchase.

Freeze-dried food has the benefit of easy storage and convenience of feeding. Naturally, there is a higher price to be paid for this convenience, but the freeze drying companies insist that the natural vitamins and minerals of these foods remain intact during processing, since no heat is used.

If tropical fish acceptance of a food is any indication of its goodness, these foods must be judged highly, since most fish eagerly devour these savory tidbits.

Any of the foods listed below can be fed to angelfish either alive, fresh, frozen, or freeze-dried. While the list does not differentiate between those foods that are impossible to feed alive, such as squid, the reader's intelligence will quickly suggest which foods will be available, practical and in which forms.

FRESH FOODS SUITABLE FOR ANGELFISH

Baby fish	Fish roe	Oysters
Beef heart	Fruit flies	Scallops
Bloodworms	Gammarus shrimp	Shrimp
Brine shrimp	Hard-boiled egg	Snail meat
Clams	Lean beef	Squid
Crab	Lobster	Tubifex worms
Crayfish	Maggots	Waterboatmen
Daphnia	Mosquito larva	White fish
Earthworms	Mussels	White worms

5. DISEASES

The problem of tropical fish diseases should be considered long before any symptoms of disease appear. As described elsewhere, a strong program of disease prevention is unquestionably superior to any attempts at curing diseases to which angelfish may succumb.

Several diseases which attack angelfish are difficult to cure and successful treatment is unusual. Fortunately, these diseases are rare and prevention is a simple matter of routine care and cleanliness.

The unsatisfactory alternative to careful preventive maintenance is treatment of diseases as they occur. The disadvantage of treatment of disease as opposed to prevention, is that medicines are frequently as hard on the fish as the disease itself. Indiscriminate overdoses of most medications are harmful and may even sterilize breeding stock or result in the deaths of those fish being treated.

Continuously recurring diseases present another problem of developing immunity to previously successful medications, requiring dosages of escalating strengths. For example, when an antibiotic is used to cure finrot, a small number of bacteria usually survive and become the foundation of a new strain which is immune to the old medication. A new, stronger medication is then sought, and unfortunately the entire process is endlessly repeated with the constant necessity of stronger and stronger drugs.

This, meanwhile, is detrimental to the fish in treatment, which must be periodically exposed to increasing shocks to the body system. Such is the disturbing paradox of antibiotics.

Strains of *Ichthyophtirius,* a disease to which angelfish usually show strong resistance, exist which are immune to standard doses of malachite green. It is obvious, then, that medication of tropical fishes should be minimized for their welfare and the practice of fish doctoring should place the primary emphasis upon disease prevention.

It must be noted equally that if it becomes necessary to treat a disease, the aquarist must seek to determine and remove the cause as well as the physical symptoms. If ich is present and induced by a cool draft, the draft should be stopped to prevent a recurrence of the problem. This is fully as important as treating the spots the fish already have. If the aquarist neglects to siphon his aquariums regularly, the result will be finrot on his best veiltailed breeders. To effect a cure of this finrot, regular siphoning must be reinstated as well as dosing the aquarium with antibiotics to cure the present infection.

Occasionally, even the most competent aquarists will face an outbreak of disease in their aquariums. Some favorite medications of the author are noted in the following paragraphs. While these medications may not produce the best results for breeders everywhere, they have proved themselves quite satisfactory on angelfish over a trial period of several years.

For external parasitic infestations, such as ich or velvet, the old treatment of quinine (used in the treatment of malaria) at a dosage of 1 grain per gallon of water works remarkably well. Treatment may be repeated after three days in stubborn cases, but one treatment is usually sufficient. Change water within one week after cure, since quinine begins to decompose. The water temperature need not be raised, but if brought up to 85 degrees F, the parasite's life cycle is accelerated and they are rapidly destroyed before the quinine has a chance to decompose in the water.

Erythromycin (25 milligrams per gallon) is usually successful in treating fungus and bacterial diseases. Aureomycin and Tetracycline are less successful, although still satisfactory remedies.

Whenever antibiotics are used, and there are many more besides those listed, the aquarist must be certain of obtaining water soluable antibiotics. Many oral antibiotic preparations currently dispensed for human consumption are unsatisfactory for aquarium use. They are designed to become effective when dissolved in human stomach acid, not water! As a general rule, but not without exception, capsules usually dissolve in water and pills usually do not. Some brands of penicillin tablets do not dissolve in water at all, therefore they are completely useless for the treatment of aquarium fish diseases.

Methylene blue and potassium permanganate (5% aqueous solution) should always be readily available to the angelfish breeder. These two medications are invaluable in treating adults, eggs, and fry alike. When bacteria blooms in the aquarium, either of these liquids will help to eliminate it without undue strain on the fishes. While exact dosages are not critical, as a guide the breeder should use about two drops of methylene blue per gallon of water or a teaspoon of potassium permanganate per 5 gallons of water. One treatment is usually sufficient, but it can be repeated once every 24 hours. The strength of the dosage of these two medications may be repeated up to three times without danger to the fish. Potassium permanganate may be used even more frequently since it rapidly breaks down in aquarium water. These medications are often helpful when it is not desired to use antibiotics. Often it is wise to attempt a cure with these two medications (one or the other) before any other treatment is tried, thus saving the antibiotics for use only as a last resort.

There are dozens of aquarium remedies commercially available for treatment of fish diseases and most of them consist of various combinations of malachite green, methylene blue, acriflavine, copper sulphate, and silver oxide. Assorted other "secret" ingredients are added to impress the layman as much as to cure the fish. One of these delightfully pompous sounding ingreients is sodium chloride. Officious sounding as it is, table salt is indeed one of the most effective aquarium remedies ever devised!

Sulpha drugs are sold to aquarists for treatment of finrot and bacterial infections. They work well at first but like antibiotics, when used repeatedly they become useless for destroying certain diseases because the parasites develop an immunity towards the drug. One effective technique is employed by treating a disease with an antibiotic first, and if necessary, to redose the disease by treatment with sulpha drugs. By alternating the treatment, the strain of pathological bacteria has less opportunity to become immune to treatment.

An important rule in treating diseases of aquarium fish is once the disease has been cured and the cause removed, it is essential to completely clean and sterilize the treated aquarium. This is a preventative maneuver, intended to destroy remaining mutant disease-causing bacteria before they begin to multiply and cause a relapse in the fish. Another reason is that medicines such as quinine and tetracycline decompose in the water, rapidly breaking down to the point of becoming toxic to the fish. It can be indescribably discouraging to be successful in curing maladies only to have the fish subsequently die from the decomposing medication.

One useful disease-preventing technique of the author is to place a half dozen eighth-inch sized silver droplets in each aquarium filter. These are wrapped in a bit of nylon to prevent loss when cleaning the filter. As the silver dissolves in the water, it tends to kill off many undesirable microscopic forms of life and thus prevent infections. Parasites find it equally difficult to thrive in water where silver is present. A couple of silver nuggets placed in the incubator jar with angelfish eggs also helps keep egg fungus to an absolute minimum!

Such silver nuggets or droplets are made from pure silver and are sold in coin shops (to silver speculators) and also in jewelry shops which supply metals to amateur jewelers. Another possible source where these silver droplets may be acquired are at various craft shops. If these are unobtainable, filings from a pure silver bar would prove equally satisfactory.

Some specific problems require specific treatments.

One common ailment of angelfish is mouth fungus. This is frequently caused by unduly frightening a mature angelfish, when netting and causes bruising of the mouth, or from damage incurred during the vigorous courting and mating activities. This disease should be anticipated and thus avoided. Care should always be used when handling mature specimens to prevent mouth damage induced by fright. If spotted early enough, the disease is easily cured, but if left to advance too long, the fish may become permanently scarred and mutilated. This may result in an inability to eat or care for eggs, rendering the fish useless for breeding and destined to waste away. Treatment is with antibiotics or sulpha drugs, either is effective.

Dosage is typically 25 milligrams per gallon for nearly all antibiotics and supha drugs, but dosage should be checked on the package if the medication has been purchased from a tropical fish dealer. If the medication is experimental, if the hobbyist is trying it for the first time, the guideline of 25 milligrams per gallon is a fine starting point. Certainly no stronger dosage should be attempted until this strength proves ineffective.

There is little to be done for tumors and lesions that do not heal, other than to destroy infected fish. The concern here should be that a strain is not being developed which is prone to tumors. When a breeding angelfish shows signs of a tumor, as a matter of practice their offspring should not be retained as breeding stock. The condition can be hereditary and is induced by too much inbreeding of a strain. While heroic measures may bring a fish through such an illness, the practicality in a semi-commerical breeding situation is far from realistic. Both the fish and the hobbyist are better off if it is quickly and painlessly destroyed. Although this may seem apathetic and heartless, the cold facts require this action. Aquarium space is always at a premium and such space as would be occupied by useless old and diseased fishes could be readily filled with young breeding stock.

One dilemma that can be easily solved is the problem of a dominant partner. When angelfish are force-mated without free choice, the unions are tenuous at best and stormy outbursts occasionally occur. One partner may attempt to kill the other. The solution is to separate the pair until the victim recovers and has gained strength. Ideally, other mates should be sought for such fish, but if a reunion is necessary, the dominant partner will usually willingly accept the return of its mate — for a time. The unhappy episode may be repeated several times, but if the aquarist is watchful and manages to intervene and save the weaker fish, no great harm is done.

Aging is one malady to which there is presently no solution. The life expectancy of breeding angelfish is relative to care, experience of the breeder, and diet given to the fish. If the novice raises angelfish to maturity and successfully breeds them for another year, without losses of breeders, he can consider himself well on the road to becoming an advanced hobbyist. Many breeders of angelfish have kept good pairs producing for up to 5 years and more, but the author's record for a single pair in production is three years, which commenced at one year of age. Extended productivity from older pairs may lead to disappointments such as smaller spawns, more fungous eggs, and a larger percentage of deformed young.

The age at which a mated pair can still be productive is primarily determined by the degree and quality of care received, but pairs over four years of age should be retired from breeding unless they are exceptionally beautiful and productive.

This chapter was composed to instill in the student of angelfish breeding a fish doctoring sense, or generalized competence in treating and preventing diseases, rather than to deal with every possible disease specifically. Since results vary widely from area to area, and information of the specific nature of fish doctoring becomes rapidly obsolete, the idea has been to foster a basic understanding of fish diseases and treatment, leaving specific experimentation to each interested individual. If anything, the primary emphasis should unquestionably be placed upon disease prevention rather than cures once diseases have struck.

6. BEGINNING TO BREED ANGELFISH

To breed angelfish, one must first begin by acquiring the necessary equipment. The minimum equipment required for breeding angelfish includes three aquariums, assorted pumps, filters, and other basic necessities which will be readily apparent to every neophyte aquarist.

Three aquariums are the minimum requirement in order to house mature fish which are beginning to pair off. If the expected pair develops, they must have their own aquarium. The third aquarium will soon be filled with the rapidly arriving spawn.

While one 30 gallon aquarium would suffice for someone only casually interested in angelfish breeding — most serious aquarists are likely to have at least three aquariums in their homes.

The main aquarium, at this stage, should be at least 30 gallons in size. This is used, as stated, to pair off all of the adult angelfish which have been raised to maturity, as explained later in this chapter. At least one 10 gallon aquarium will be required to house the first pair. Subsequent pairs will also require separate housing, but that can be worked out later.

The breeder, depending upon his ambitions, can now stop with the acquisition of a single pair, or he can continue pairing off his mature fish. If desired, he can dispose of all remaining fish and use the now freed large tank to raise one spawn of fry. This is extremely limited production and can never amount to anything so gradiose as to expect a profit. On the other hand, it can permit the novice breeder to test his wings and see if his notions of fish breeding can be put into practice.

Once the breeder determines that he is going to breed angelfish as a hobby, the next step is the acquisition of several more aquariums. Since the combined total of baby angelfish produced from one good pair will equal about 2,000 fish every two months — birth to marketing period — it can be appreciated that at least half a dozen 29 or 30 gallon aquariums are going to be necessary per producing pair!

Going back a bit, let us assume that the hobbyist has just purchased his initial 30 gallon aquarium and 8 or 10 beautiful angelfish to inhabit it. The number should not actually be above 7 fish, but at this point we will assume that a couple are going to expire during the 6 months raising period.

With about 8 silver, black lace, or marble angelfish, which are best because of hardiness and marketability, the hobbyist sets about raising these fish for breeding. These three varietes are superior to all others presently available and provide the hobbyist ample opportunity to perfect his breeding techniques before advancing to the delicate veiltails.

Black lace angelfish are undoubtedly the best choice since a single pair of this strain will produce three varieties which all find a ready market: silver, black lace, and blacks.

While it may sound logical for the breeder to go out and purchase an already mated pair, in order to thrust oneself full-scale into breeding angelfish, this is by far the least wise course of action.

It is equally tempting to purchase nearly mature specimens in the hope that they will pair off soon. Impatience is common enough in every form of endeavor, but that does not mean it is wise. Half grown angelfish and mated pairs have a previously unknown history, and to put it in the blunt words of the German master aquarist Ferdinand Cochu: "They are fish with a past, not a future!" The care of these fish may have been poor, they may have had unknown diseases, they may have even been sterilized. The exception, naturally, is to purchase your breeding stock from an expert breeder who specializes in the supplying of breeding stock to novice aquarists; but these are few enough today.

Some probabilities that one should avoid when buying mated pairs include: 1) old fish, no longer productive; 2) highly infertile male with limited hatches; 3) flighty, mismatched, nervous pairs; 4) production of a high percentage of deformed or off colored young.

Since buying an already mated pair can prove deceptive, since the above points might not be easily discernible to the beginning fish breeder, it is obviously wiser to develop the patience to raise one's own pairs.

The principal benefit derived from the purchase of young fish is that they will become well adapted to the habits and care of the aquarist who will be breeding them. The probable reward for the patient aquarist will be enviable success.

Raising young angelfish to adulthood is satisfying and provides time for consideration before one becomes overwhelmed by the awesome production of thousands of fry which is entirely unexpected. Suddenly raging full throttle in angelfish production leaves a hiatus of necessary experience and can lead to unanticipated and frustratingly difficult problems.

Once the future breeding stock has been purchased and housed in a suitable aquarium, it is time to develop nutritional and maintenance habits as previously explained. These important habits should be learned correctly from the beginning, since bad habits are difficult to correct once they become ingrained in daily practice.

Provided all goes well, before long — usually 10 months from birth — it will become time to pair off the angelfish for breeding. It is at this point that many sincere and dedicated hobbyists fail miserably in producing mated pairs. Amazingly, this can be attributed simply to trying too hard.

The basic practice in pairing off angelfish is the same whether a single pair is desired or the continuous pairing of mature angelfish is the goal.

The method begins by stocking a 30 gallon aquarium with five or six mature angelfish. Using more than six fish practically guarantees failure. The critical number is six in this instance because any more fish present in a 30 gallon aquarium will severely inhibit any courtship and mating activities.

By placing too many mature angelfish in the pairing aquarium, the ambitious hobbyist hopes for a shortcut to produce four or five pairs instead of one or two. This effort, unfortunately, is always destined to failure. When angelfish are too crowded, they develop a common identity and lose all interest in pairing off and reproducing. Because territorial boundaries cannot be established by potential breeding pairs, they simply stop all attempts at mating. There is just too much conflict if crowded conditions are allowed and the result is no pairs and no spawnings!

With only five or six angelfish in the aquarium, however, the experienced breeder always provides at least four spawning sites and ends up with two pairs within a matter of only a few days. The extra sites prevent needless squabbling among the males over suitable locations to claim a territory.

The fish are then fed frequently and heavily to ensure the development of eggs in the females. The aquarium is watched carefully for signs of pairing off.

These signs are unmistakable to anyone who has bred angelfish. The male and female, having locked jaws and determined their mutual compatibility, commence defending their chosen site against any and all intrusions by their neighbors. Often a second pairing will occur among the remaining fish, much to the delight of the aquarist.

If mature angelfish are not too crowded and are set-up as indicated, and as long as both males and females are present, pairing off will continue. This strong natural drive of angelfish is actually quite difficult to inhibit, as evidenced by the common occurrence of angelfish matings and spawnings in home community aquariums.

The next step in the pairing process is to remove each pair to a separate aquarium for permanent maintenance. While it is commonly believed that a pair must be captured and removed in the same net, at the same time, to prevent breaking up of the pair, such information is not founded on facts. Such contorted acrobatics are required to accomplish this stunt, it is wiser to calmly remove each fish separately to avoid damaging them.

The misconception that a pair will not remate if netted separately probably originated from a breeder having netted the wrong fish when netting a pair out one at a time. Obviously, such fish would not remate since they had never mated in the first place. Netting a pair together might logically prevent this mistake from occurring, but it is not true that a pair of angelfish netted separately will not remate.

The ideal way to capture and remove a mated pair is by using two nets. The first net, a large one, is used to isolate the pair from all the other fish in the aquarium. The second net, a medium sized net, is then used to carefully net out each fish without causing undue excitement. Slow steady movements are best.

If the pair has already spawned, the spawn can be placed in the aquarium with the pair if it is desired that they raise the fry. They may not eat them, but if they do, the next spawn will be all the larger. The recommended course of action is to remove the spawn to a separate hatching jar and raise them separately. The next spawn can be raised naturally with the parents, if desired, after the pair has settled down.

Pairs can be permanently housed in bare 10 gallon aquariums equipped with nothing more than a box filter and a slate strip. (Plastic strips are almost as good.) The slate is secured at about a 45 degree angle opposite the corner with the filter.

The permanent breeding tank should be away from areas where unexpected disturbances might occur. If a special room is available for the fish, it is desirable to keep unnecessary traffic in the fishroom to an absolute minimum. More elaborate installations will be examined under the small scale commercial production chapters.

7. THE SPAWNING

An angelfish spawning is always interesting to observe; the graceful movements of the complete spawning ritual are unforgettable to those who have seen it.

A sure sign of an impending spawning occurs two days prior to the actual event. The pair becomes very territorial and defensive toward all disturbances occurring near their aquarium, especially in the vicinity of the chosen spawning site. An angelfish's territory seems to radiate approximately 12 inches in every direction from the site. This will vary between pairs, and in nature this territorial area may be even larger. It is unlikely, however, that natural territories could be much larger, since straying too far from the spawn would jeopardize the helpless fry by predators approaching from another direction. Whereas a typical 10 gallon aquarium does not allow for as much territory as would normally be defended, pairs are content with the reduced area.

As spawning approaches, the pair will busily begin to clean their site and test it for strength and suitability to receive the forthcoming spawn. If the site proves unsuitable, the breeder may intervene and influence some pairs to choose a more satisfactory location. Some pairs may stubbornly decide to spawn only on a heater tube, the aquarium wall, or even a filter tube, in preference to the slate provided. If they begin to clean a different site than desired by the hobbyist, the wisest course of action is to move the slate near the position the pair has chosen. The pair will usually willingly accept this new arrangement. If not, suspect something wrong with the spawning surface supplied. It may be too slick, too dirty, or simply not strong enough to satisfy the pair. Call it instinct, accumulated hereditary experience, or intelligence; it remains a fact that pairs will sometimes choose a location different than provided in a seemingly logical manner. It may be because of unsuitable lighting, insufficient water circulation, or a sense of insecurity, but the pair will manage to find their own suitable site if the one provided by the hobbyist is not satisfactory.

Cooperating with the pair is the safest procedure, and the only alternative to failure. Move the slate if necessary. That will ensure that the spawn will be deposited conveniently upon the slate which has been provided.

One day prior to the spawning, the pair's breeding tubes will begin to descend, only slightly at first, then finally extending as much as a fourth of an inch before spawning commences. It is at this moment when positive sexing becomes possible.

Make it a point to determine the sex of breeding angelfish at this time. This is essential for future reference. If a mate is later lost and needs to be replaced, or if it is desired to fix a new strain by selective breeding, it is critical to know the sex of one's breeding fish.

Sexing angelfish is easily accomplished when breeding tubes are extended. Since the female's tube delivers the eggs to the site, and the male's tube supplies only the milt, the female's tube is naturally the larger. Her tube is also wider and blunter than the male's tube, which is narrow and somewhat pointed.

When the spawning begins, the female will usually make about a dozen trial runs up the slate. During this preparatory activity, the male will carefully defend the surrounding area while watchfully observing whether the female has begun to deposit any eggs. He senses when he is needed and rarely participates in the female's eggless trials. The trial passes seem to stimulate the female into the process of egg release. This preliminary can become quite unnerving to the inexperienced angelfish breeder, who will erroneously conclude that the female is egg-bound. Any valiant, but misguided, heroics could, at this point, ruin a perfectly good spawning. The rule then, is hands off, and be patient.

Now the female will begin to glide slowly and deliberately up the slate, gracefully depositing eggs in a single, straight row, rarely overlapping a single egg. With a fine and delicate sense of touch, she will interlay up to 1,000 eggs in a two or three inch square area. The spacing is essential, since too close proximity of the eggs permits fungus to spread more rapidly, while a too wide spacing requires extra fanning and guarding. Fortunately, the female knows instinctively how to place her eggs, so the aquarist has little cause for concern.

It is extremely important to avoid startling a spawning pair, which would distract them from their spawning activities. A single unfertilized row of eggs, numbering only thirty perhaps, will rapidly endanger an additional two hundred eggs in the immediate vicinity. Absolute privacy during the spawning act must therefore be strictly enforced. An excessively nervous pair, suffering from constant disturbances during spawnings, may actually go into severe shock and even die as a result of it. While this is, admittedly, a rare occurrence, it has happened more than once in the past.

The normal duration of an angelfish spawning is nearly 2 hours. If normal care and precautions have been taken, a fine spawn can be expected when the breeding pair are finally approached by the hobbyist.

Many successful angelfish breeders keep notes of the dates of each spawning recorded on each pair's aquarium. Whatever the spawning frequency of a pair, when part of the water is replaced with fresh dechlorinated water on the day spawning is due, usually the pair will maintain their schedule. If a pair repeatedly spawns every ten days, for example, the breeder need only change 50% of the water in that tank on the morning of the tenth day to induce spawning. Some pairs are 14 day cycle spawners, others will spawn as frequently as every seven days. With experience, one can soon begin to anticipate the arrival of nearly every spawn. Conversely, a spawn may be postponed a day or so, if necessary, by simply not changing part of the water. Once pairs have become accustomed to having some water changed just prior to spawning, this can be used advantageously to regulate daily spawn production.

Too many spawnings occurring on a particular day, certainly a delightful problem to face, could be regulated to produce a more manageable delivery program. All that is required for such control are accurate records and habitual water changes preceding spawning.

If overproduction occurs, as it sometimes does when one becomes really proficient, feeding the excess eggs to the parents produces extremely large spawns immediately thereafter (after the normal elapse of time.) The best procedure is to scrape the eggs from the slate and feed them to hungry breeding stock due to spawn soon. This will produce larger, stronger spawns with less likelihood of egg fungus destroying the batch.

There is always the risk that pairs may develop a taste for their eggs, but normally a pair's strong parental instincts restrain them for at least twenty-four hours after each new spawn, which gives the aquarist sufficient time to remove the eggs to the safety of the incubator jar.

Certain pairs will habitually spawn at certain times of day. Some prefer spawning at sunrise, other pairs always spawn at dusk. If notes are taken of each pair's habits, spawning can be accurately anticipated. The breeder is thus ready when expected spawns arrive.

8. ALLOWING PARENTAL CARE

Most hobbyists wish to witness personally the fascinating parental care demonstrated by breeding angelfish at least once. Witnessing the family scene is both instructive and desirable for a thorough understanding of the art of angelfish propagation. By carefully observing the behavior of the parent fish, the hobbyist can readily comprehend the significance of the procedures necessary for success in the artificial egg incubation process.

Aside from the purely educational consideration, natural angelfish breeding is endlessly entertaining to the hobbyist and his family. Hours pass quickly while studying the interesting behavior and intelligent actions of a mated pair with their fry.

The probability of a pair raising a spawn to maturity is roughly one in ten (10%). That is to say, an average pair will raise only one spawn in ten. Individual pairs may average slightly more, but overall, the figure of 10% is accurate when considering the average home spawning.

With careful attention to some of the variable factors involved, this percentage of spawns reared naturally can be vastly improved.

While angelfish have previously been attributed with the ability to predetermine a spawn's survival quotient and other vaguely described characteristics, this is hardly likely. It is far more reasonable to suppose that variable environmental factors in each instance contribute either positively or negatively to a pair's actions. Assuming that a mated pair cannot accurately predict the physical qualities of a spawn before it has developed, were this possible it would border on psychic phenomenon, then the stimulus prompting the pair to eat their spawn must be external. Thus, a logical examination of existing external factors can enormously improve the probability of a spawn being reared.

One factor which certainly causes many spawns to be devoured is the presence of other fish in the aquarium. Other fish visible in another nearby aquarium are equally unnerving to breeding pairs with a spawn of young angelfish to defend. Under such continuous stresses, few pairs will endure the protective activity seemingly necessary and in consequence, they will eat their eggs in desperation.

The overall predictable environmental tranquility sensed by a mated pair primarily determines their behavior. The degree of security felt by a pair is directly related to the probability of their rearing a spawn.

It is just when the pair spawns that the hobbyist thoughtlessly abandons carefully established habits and rituals and flagrantly violates the security sense of the mated pair. The hobbyist intrudes upon the privacy of the breeding pair night and day, arriving unexpectedly and acting erratically. Feeding schedules are apt to be disregarded and room lighting habits abandoned. The pair, obviously at the point of distraction, will experience the complete breakdown of their secure environment and devour their spawn.

It must now be clear that habits and schedules are to be carefully maintained if a pair is expected to raise a spawn. To ensure success, the hobbyist must react by displaying little apparent interest in the spawn and ignoring the activities of the breeding pairs.

The characteristic threatening gestures of the parents must equally be respected. If a pair senses themselves to be ineffectual in protecting their fry, they are likely to eat them. This is avoided by refraining from exciting the pair. If the pair charges at the glass in defiance of one's presence, it is advisable to back off several feet. Through this action, the confidence of the pair is inclined to increase rather than to be frustrated. Whenever a pair becomes noticeably agitated, a retreat of several steps reassures them and improves their mutual confidence in one another.

The location of the spawning aquarium must be carefully predetermined to ensure minimum disturbance to the pair, yet afford the hobbyist maximum opportunities for observation of the family. Once the hobbyist develops an affected attitude of indifference when near the pair, any normally suitable locations would be satisfactory. A high traffic area should be avoided unless all passersby are instructed to purposefully ignore the breeding aquarium. Abnormal interest shown in the activities of an inexperienced breeding pair is likely to unnerve them, resulting in the loss of the fry.

A considerably important factor relative to success with a breeding pair is the size of the aquarium used. While fewer young are always raised by a pair than would be likely if the eggs were incubated artificially, the number of young a pair will raise is determined by the size of the breeding tank.

In repeated experiments conducted by the author, no pair ever raised more than 55 young in a ten gallon aquarium, although as many as 400 have been hatched out. The number 50, with a 10% variable, was consistently chosen by several pairs allowed to rear their own young. Such seemingly intelligent decisions not to overproduce were almost uncanny. It became apparent there was a sense of environment and that the aquarium would not support a larger number without self destruction for all. The powerful survival instinct of nature was obviously at work.

Still another factor determining success is the availability of several possible spawning sites. Since a spawn is to be intentionally reared by the parents, an aquarium larger than 10 gallons is necessary. Several spawning locations are easier to provide in a larger aquarium and the sense of security of a breeding pair is thereby increased.

If natural breeding is to be attempted, an aquarium of approximately 30 gallons is most suitable. In an aquarium of this size, four or five likely spawning sites should be provided to offer a choice to the pair. Having chosen their own location, the pair are more likely to raise their spawn.

Finally, when a pair is rearing a family, they should be fed the same amount of food as their pre-spawning conditioning. The continuous activity necessary to guard and control an average spawn expends enormous amounts of energy and increases the appetite. Considering that baby fish are the choice diet of angelfish, every effort must be made to keep the parents well fed to reduce cannibalism.

If one partner of the angelfish becomes less attentive and watchful, the other quickly senses it. He or she will attempt to peck and scold the offending partner. If the attempts to reform the disinterested partner fail, serious combat can ensue which ends with the young being devoured. This situation is rare enough if the pair have chosen each other from among a group, while forced matings frequently experience such conflicts. Logically, spawns should only be left with parents which have naturally mated rather than in cases where a male and female have been induced to breed.

Parental care commences moments after spawning is completed.

The female begins to fan the eggs and keep an attentive eye as the eggs develop. The male, meanwhile, begins his faithful vigil. At this point, the normally shy angelfish become fearless in the defense of their family.

Both parents will guard the eggs and both will fan them, but fanning appears to be the principle duty of the female, while the male usually assumes the post of lookout. This continues through the egg and alevin stage, with the mother delicately caring for her brood. Although the fry hatch by themselves, the mother seems to sense the proper moment when the embryos are ready to emerge and often assists the alevins in freeing themselves from the shell with a combination of pecking and blowing.

Once the alevins have hatched, parental care intensifies; the pair becomes almost feverish in their anxious, purposeful movements. Pairs often move the newly born alevins to a new location, previously investigated and prepared.

Presumably, this activity is determined by the sense of security of the pair and the availability of secondary sites affording adequate safety for the avevins.

If the ability to choose logically a spawning site is attributed to the pair (I use "logically" in the broadest possible sense), it makes little sense that they would transfer the alevins to a less suitable location simply as a precautionary measure. It seems more likely that a pair which feels their young are threatened at the original site, often by nothing more than an excitable hobbyist, will attempt to hide their young.

One unlikely reason that the fry are moved is to ensure they are washed by the mouths of the parents. Since incubated fry require no such washings to ensure their survival, and since all pairs do not wash or move their fry, the assumption is probably incorrect. The churning action of the parental maw full of young simply allows fresh oxygenated water to reach the young at all times. This practical action prevents suffocation of the fry. Normal respiration, with a mouthful of wriggling alevins, is certainly impossible as well, since without the characteristic chewing motion, the alevins might either become stuck in the parent's gills or clumsily expelled through the operculum.

When the fry finally become free swimming, both parents assume equal watchfulness. Normal positioning places the parental couple tail to tail, several inches apart with the fry sandwiched between. This standard guarding has two advantages. Straying fry are rapidly spotted and retrieved without a moments lapse from the guard duty; and secondly, all directions are covered to reveal any lurking intruders.

When an occasional fry ventures too far from the school, a tireless parent quickly captures the runaway by "eating" him and then spitting him back into the group.

Again the churning motion of the mouth is observed and the author likes to speculate privately that the young are being taught the lesson: To venture from the school results in being eaten. While this is not the thought-out intention of the parent, being suddenly engulfed in a large fish's mouth must graphically illustrate to a wandering fry that to survive, a little fish had best remain in school!

Aside from the instructional and entertaining reasons for letting the pair raise a spawn, there is another more practical reason to allow a pair to raise their spawn. The fifty or more fry raised by their parents can be kept for future breeding.

It is yet to be proven that naturally raised fish make better breeding stock since fish psychology is a vastly unexplored subject. If however, other animals become disoriented and confused without proper parental care, it can be speculated that angelfish would behave similarly. Therefore, the natural parental care of angelfish would result in healthier stock.

9. THE DEVELOPING SPAWN

Having a spawn of eggs deposited on a slate does not insure success, but it is simply the first step in the series of events leading to a marketable school of angelfish. This chapter will guide the reader so that success will not be simply a possibility, but rather, a certainty. Success will be the result if the reader considers each step carefully.

Many aquarists have, at one time or another, been unexpectedly blessed with a spawn of angelfish eggs in the home community aquarium. It is another matter, however, to successfully raise 300 to 500 baby angels from spawning to the size of a quarter with minimum losses and perfect health. This is what separates the professionals from the vast majority of neophyte aquarists.

Available information concerning proper procedures is often sketchy and incomplete. Many initial efforts lead to unnecessary failure because the basic principles and procedures are not clearly understood. Once mastered, however, breeding angelfish becomes almost mechanical in its simplicity. Common sense, as is so often the case, is the best guide.

The first step, when dealing with a new spawn, is to remove it carefully from the parent fish and place it in an incubator jar or other container. A container of about one gallon is ideal for receiving new spawns. Easily handled, easily cleaned, and requiring little space, the one gallon jar has proven to be the most suitable receptacle during the first week of care. In such a small volume of water, the required chemical treatment is kept to a minimum and the eggs are easily viewed to monitor their progress.

The slate or plastic strip should have been carefully measured in advance to ensure that it will fit into the hatching container. It is awkward and disheartening to remove the spawn from the parents and suddenly discover that the slate will not fit into the jar!

The location of the container should be away from strong lighting, loud noises, excessive activity, and undue temperature variations. Failure to carefully avoid such factors may not always be fatal to eggs or alevins, but moderation and stability are requirements for continuous success.

Angelfish eggs will hatch in almost any reasonable pH/water hardness combination that the parents live in. If the parents are living and thriving in the area water, do not alter the water in which the fry will be hatched. Unless faced with repeated failure, use natural water to rear the angelfish alevins and fry. Natural water that is of a pH lower than 7.8 and less than 180 ppm hardness will produce strong healthy angelfish when the parents have received proper care.

One technique for attaining suitable water is to draw fresh tap water just prior to removal of the eggs from the parents' aquarium. This water is then dechlorinated and a fungicide is added. The chlorine has killed most bacteria and fungous spores present in the water and it is in a near-perfect state to receive the eggs. When the chlorine has been neutralized immediately prior to the addition of the eggs, the hobbyist must then check to ensure that the temperatures are equal between the aquarium and the jar.

The addition of standard dyes, such as methylene blue or acriflavine, gives the advantage of having little initial bacterial activity which aids significantly in retarding egg fungus. Any slight residual chlorine is harmless to the eggs and quickly dissipates when the water is properly aerated. Even untreated chlorinated water does not kill the eggs unless it is so strong that it is repulsive to drink. The water can be aerated for an hour before the addition of the eggs, if desired, and the bubbling action helps remove any other gasses which may be present in the tap water. It also tends to aid the water in absorbing oxygen which may be lacking in the water.

When the airstone is placed in the jar, the aeration must be steady and even. The airstone must be in place prior to introducing the eggs, since banging about the jar once the eggs are inside is sure to dislodge many of them. Previously unused one-inch airstones are best. It is attached to a spotlessly clean airline tubing. Although it is possible to boil and reuse airline tubing, it is best to use a small section of new tubing with each spawn. This prevents the possibility of forgetting and using contaminated tubing which may introduce egg fungus into the hatchery jar.

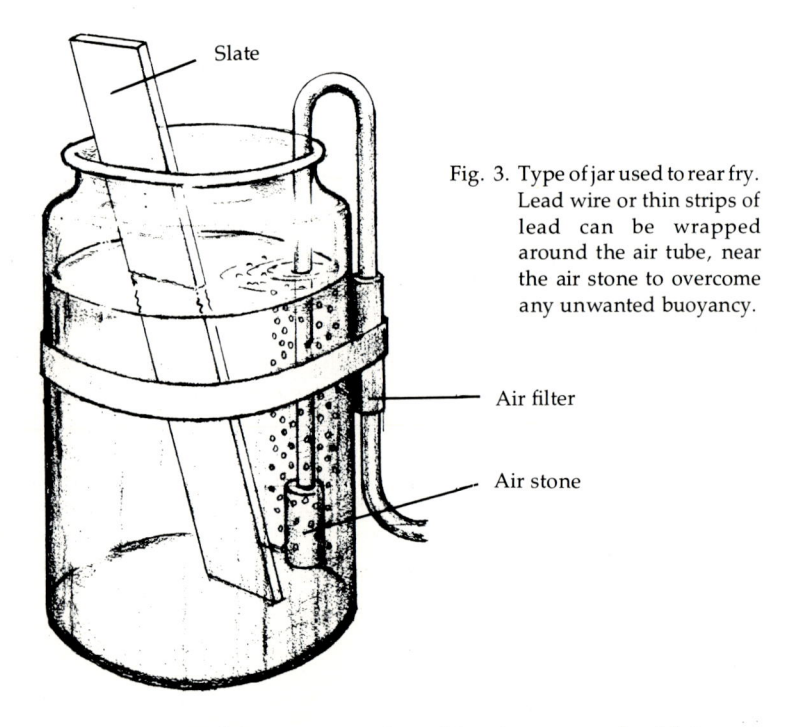

Fig. 3. Type of jar used to rear fry. Lead wire or thin strips of lead can be wrapped around the air tube, near the air stone to overcome any unwanted buoyancy.

At the base of the airstone, the tubing is wrapped with two or three strips of pure lead plant-weights which have been carefully cleaned beforehand. This will keep the stone submerged by reducing buoyancy.

A section of 'U' shaped rigid tubing can be connected to the airstone inside of the jar. This helps to keep the airstone in place and allows a certain amount of control once the eggs are in place.

The airstone and tubing are held in place by a strong rubberband or string tied around the outside of the jar.

Next comes the water treatment. There is no single best medication to prevent egg fungus. The best known and most commercially marketed preparation is methylene blue, but it is not any better than silver oxide, copper sulphate, or acriflavine. The accompanying chart gives the correct strength and dosages commonly used for angelfish eggs. In some areas a slightly stronger dosage may be necessary, in other regions a weaker dose will suffice. There are no hard and fast rules concerning water treatment to combat egg fungus, and this accounts for the great deal of contradictory information prevalent among enthusiasts. While one account will recommend 3 drops of 5% methylene blue, another breeding account may state that only silver oxide produces satisfactory results. There is little sense in attempting to make a judgment regarding which is the best because of the many variable factors which affect the outcome of each treatment. No intelligent conclusion could be reached without the aid of strict laboratory research.

MEDICATION	STRENGTH	DROPS PER GALLON
Methylene Blue	5%	8
Copper Sulphate	3%	1
Silver Oxide	5%	8
Acriflavine	5%	2
Malachite Green	5%	2

(It must be stressed that this chart is only a guideline upon which the aquarist may develop his own best formulae.)

To determine which chemical is most suitable for his area, the hobbyist will probably have to do a little home experimentation. One must not always blame the medication for failure, however. The fault could just as readily be due to improper water preparation, unclean conditions, or a lazy breeder male.

Anti-funguous medications are only the final precaution in a series of positive actions leading to ultimate success. If all has been properly prepared, there is little necessity for medication except to reassure the hobbyist and increase the hatch somewhat. If precautions have been half-hearted and slack, however, no amount of medication is going to ensure success, since failure is inevitable. In the proper perspective, it is seen that the use of dyes and metal salts is simply a means of raising large numbers of fry, rather than insurance against failure. Once this is clearly understood, once the hobbyist shifts his dependency to himself rather than to anti-fungus medicines, there is little likelihood of failure.

If met with consistent failure and the water is suspected, then it may be carefully altered to meet individual requirements. Since angelfish live naturally in rainwater acidified by decomposing vegetation, the ideal water for angelfish eggs and alevins would seem to be rainwater. The only problem of using rainwater is that in most populated areas of the world, fresh rainwater may be dangerously polluted. It certainly is not satisfactory for rearing delicate baby fish. During a heavy downpour, suitable water, which is relatively clean, may be trapped by waiting several minutes before placing out any traps. Even water from heavily industrialized areas may be greatly improved by filtering through charcoal for several days. One or two trials will quickly reveal whether using rainwater will be feasible.

If local water proves to be unsatisfactory, boiled unpolluted river or lake water is often better. It is a sad commentary on our civilization that unpolluted lakes and streams are a rarity. If this water is filtered for several days through a bed of charcoal, even mildly polluted river water can usually be rendered suitable. The water should always be boiled to kill undetectable microorganisms.

Barring the above as sources of soft acid water, tap water can be chemically altered. A miniature water softener can be constructed from a filter and some water softening resins. Once the water is softened, it is no problem to acidify it. Most enthusiasts mistakenly attempt to acidify water before they soften it, but the minerals present in the hard water tend to constantly revert the properties of the water toward alkaline. Once the water is demineralized, however, the addition of minute amounts of hydrochloric acid will rapidly adjust the pH to the desired level.

Bacterial and fungus spores do not grow or multiply well in soft acid water. Water with a pH near 6.4 is very suitable for eggs and developing alevins. Bacterial growths are naturally retarded in this manner and the developing embryos are thus given a measure of protection.

In soft water, the mucus thread attached to the head of the alevin, which holds him suspended in the water from the slate, is stronger and does not disintegrate as rapidly as it does in hard water. The extra strength of this thread in soft water helps the alevin remain suspended in the water longer, thus avoiding unclean conditions which may develop on the bottom of the hatching jar. The alevins' early muscular development is also accelerated and clean water is constantly all around them as opposed to their resting on the bottom where dirt accumulates.

In nature, the thread keeps the alevins in a group at one location. No doubt this aids the parents immensely in their parental duties. In hard water, it is not surprising that angelfish allowed to rear their own young quickly tire of the task when the young continually fall helplessly to the bottom of the tank where they must be endlessly retrieved.

In the hatching container, the hard alkaline water weakens this mucus thread and causes the fry to fall helplessly to the bottom of the jar. In itself, this is not a serious problem, but fungused eggs and other debris rapidly accumulate on the bottom of the nursery as well. This situation becomes dangerous to the fry since they may become diseased from unclean surroundings. The choice must be made between the extra effort of supplying soft water to the nursery or simply allowing the fry to hatch and develop in hard water. This will untimately be determined by the degree of success that the hobbyist achieves.

Since the natural habitat of angelfish consists of soft acid water, by reproducing natural water conditions better results are quite probable.

Once the proper water conditions are produced, the egg laden slate is placed in the jar, the eggs facing downward. Since they are adhesive, there is little danger of any eggs falling off the slate. Placing the eggs downward has a definite purpose. When they face up, debris and fungus easily settles upon them. But by placing the egg-side down, debris falls away from the eggs. Gravity is therefore employed rather than fought.

Position the airstone beside the slate, never directly under the eggs. A gentle stream of bubbles sent trickling upward beside the slate aerates the eggs without disturbing them. Beginners often place the airstone beneath the eggs bubbling full force. This smashes the eggs about like a thousand miniature ping-pong balls! The purpose of the airstone is to circulate the water near the eggs, not to bathe them in air.

The jar, with airstone and slate inside, is now covered with a loose fitting plastic bag. Since fungous spores and bacteria can be airborne, and can enter the jar at the water surface, such action helps thwart contamination. Locate the airpump in a clean area and install a small air line filter cartridge as well. A dusty pump site must be avoided. The floor is often a poor choice for this reason. Seemingly unimportant and often overlooked precautions as these could noticeably improve the percentage of hatching eggs from 40% to 95%.

Some eggs inevitably become fungus covered, but do not despair. Whatever is done, never try to pick off fungous eggs with a needle. Attempting to pick off angelfish eggs is a futile business and should never be tried. While the idea of removing dead eggs seems logical, one need only attempt it once to realize the worthlessness of this idea. Unless one possesses the steady hands of a neurosurgeon, attempting the removal of fungous eggs can destroy an entire spawn.

The eggs are so closely arranged that any attempt to remove the fungous eggs inevitably contaminates at least ten times the number of them already dead. Because fungous eggs burst easily, the idea of picking off dead eggs is little short of preposterous. If a dead egg bursts when attempting to remove it, the resulting visible spray of fungus will destroy not less than twenty eggs in the immediate vicinity, contaminating them within seconds.

Removing the spawn from the water to work them over with a needle is equally foolhardy. Nature never intended fungous angelfish eggs to be removed or even touched. The action of picking off fungous eggs to protect a spawn is self-defeating since the result is the opposite of what is intended.

Angelfish rarely pick off fungous eggs from a spawn when they are allowed to rear a batch. Any observation of angels seemingly removing bad eggs is likely nothing more than random pecking at the spawning site. The parents engage in this activity constantly when tending their eggs, but they are removing random specks of dirt, not contaminated eggs. At times an infertile egg may be accidentally devoured, but it is far from a general practice of picking off all bad eggs.

It is likely that many hobbyists have observed that their slates have been picked clean of bad eggs, but this is due, in the author's experience, from the pair eating fungous eggs after all of the viable eggs have hatched. It seems that the angelfish themselves do not wish to risk removing bad eggs until all of their offspring have safely hatched!

A fungous fish egg, if left alone, will not contaminate the rest of the spawn. An infertile egg which has never commenced development is little danger to the rest of the spawn since the egg shell membrane holds intact the contaminants while the remaining fertile eggs develop. This is nature's means of protecting the spawn.

Once the fry have hatched, the most difficult phase of rearing a spawn is completed. The fry are most susceptible when they are eggs. Once beyond this stage, with their basic requirements satisfied, they are easily raised and remarkably hardy.

Quite frequently novice aquarists fail in their breeding attempts at this point, just when success seems certain. Novice angelfish breeders, seeing one or two of the alevins break loose and dart aimlessly about the nursery, immediately misinterpret this as a sign that the young are free-swimming. They feed the babies too soon, which kills the fry. After hatching, the embryonic alevins do not eat for approximately five days, and the food they are so generously fed does nothing but kill them.

The dying brine shrimp or microworms simply settle to the bottom of the jar among the fry. As the food decomposes, the fry become diseased and die quickly. For this reason, newly hatched brine shrimp should never be fed to the alevins before the sixth day from the spawning date, and often not until the seventh day after spawning.

Angelfish eggs average about 48 hours to hatch and five days to become free-swimming after hatching, but this is relative to the water temperature. At temperatures above 76 degrees F. the fry develop at a more rapid rate, while at cooler temperatures the development is retarded. As long as the temperature remains stable and the range is between 72 and 78 degrees F., there is little cause for alarm if the fry take somewhat longer before hatching or becoming free-swimming.

The first meal should never be given until the fry swarm up en masse. This does not mean one or two ambitious baby angelfish venturing about the water. It means that all of the fry must be up and swimming as a group. Without a doubt, this is the most common misinterpretation of breeding information made by novice aquarists, and premature feedings are unfortunately devastatingly fatal to fry.

Both Utah and San Francisco Bay brine shrimp are perfectly satisfactory for young angelfish. Microworms are also suitable. When brine shrimp is used, it is important that they be fed immediately after hatching. Once brine shrimp hatch, they begin growing and they quickly absorb their yolk sack, which is their principal nutritional value to the young angelfish. Therefore, the nauplii must be fed within hours of hatching.

The first meal should be a light feeding and carefully administered to the fry in the hatching container. The fry should be kept and fed in their small container for another two days to ensure they get a healthy start. By feeding them in the jar, they are always in close proximity to their food. If placed immediately in a large aquarium, large amounts of brine shrimp would be required to ensure that the fry were always able to find enough food. In the small confines of the jar, the fry find their food more readily and less live food is required. Care must always be exercised to avoid overfeeding which would rapidly pollute the unfiltered jar.

After two days, it is advisable to relocate the fry to a small intermediate container. This can be a container which holds three gallons and is furnished with a sponge filter. The purpose of this container is again to ensure that the fry are always close to their food supply. If they are not overfed, the fry can be kept in this intermediate container for another week before they must be placed in a larger aquarium.

The intermediate container need not be elaborate. A plastic dishpan or plastic storage box of suitable dimensions is all that is required. The only requisites are that it hold water and be of a non-toxic material.

Filtration for the fry throughout the first month need be nothing more elaborate than the so-called sponge filters. The main benefit in these is that they do not suck up the baby fish or their food. Other filters are at a disadvantage for fry, since they can be easily sucked into almost any other type. Even undergravel filters will suck a spawn of angelfish into the gravel if medium or coarse gravel is used.

Sponge filters can easily be constructed by the use of a small plastic tube placed within a larger one in which small pin holes are bored. A piece of sponge rubber is fitted around the larger tube and an airline attached to the smaller tube. The bottom of the large tube is capped with another small piece of sponge and the entire filter is submerged into the baby tank. It may need to be weighted with a lead sinker, but this simple, rustic filter is extremely effective and protects the fry from being sucked up.

An option is to place the fry in another intermediate aquarium, such as a 10 gallon aquarium, until they are large enough to be counted and placed in large rearing aquariums. This is particularly useful when fish such as black lace are being bred, which must be sorted anyway.

The angelfish will remain in this intermediate sized aquarium for another two weeks. By this age, now four weeks old, the fry can safely be netted, counted, sorted, and set out in large aquariums where they will remain until ready to market.

Angelfish fry can be ready to sell five weeks from the time they become free-swimming. (The word "sell" is used, since throughout this book it has been assumed that the hobbyist intends to sell at least a portion of the angelfish he has raised.) To market an angelfish at five weeks from the first meal takes con-

Fig. 4. Home made sponge filter.

Plastic tube

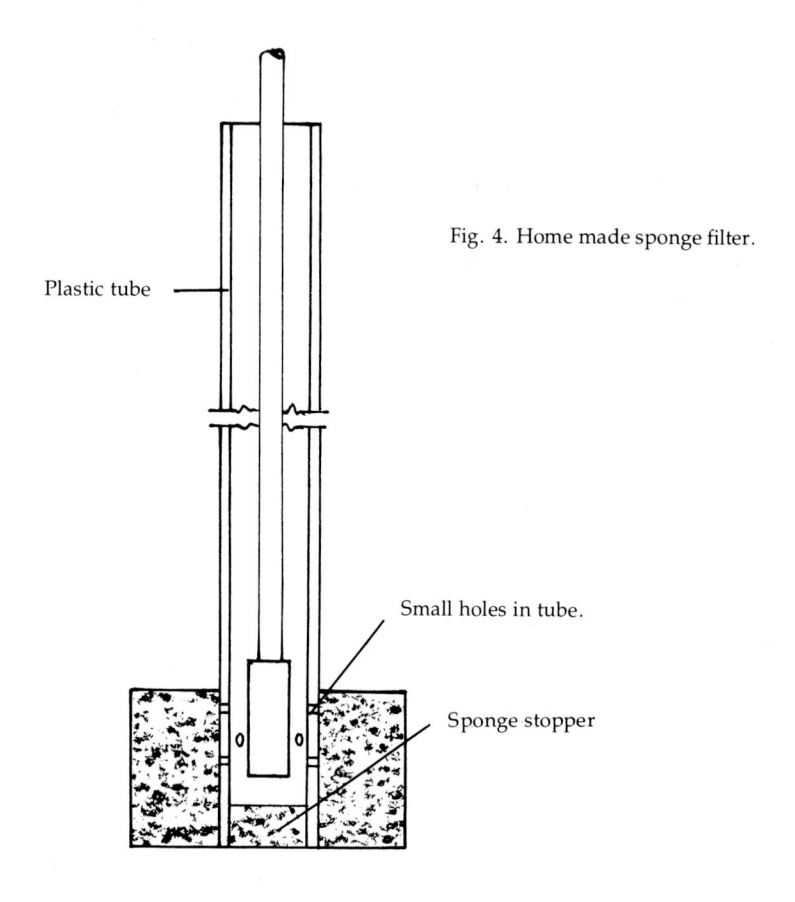

Small holes in tube.

Sponge stopper

siderable dedication and much work. To accomplish such rapid growth, frequent feedings of live brine shrimp and immaculate cleanliness of the rearing aquarium are essential.

For maximized growth, the fry are kept on an 18-hour day. This daily period of light ensures that maximum growth is realized. To benefit from the lengthened period of light in the 24-hour cycle, frequent feedings throughout the period are required.

Five daily feedings for the developing fry are just enough. If a schedule is devised which ensures maximum convenience and efficiency, five feedings daily need not be burdensome. If the fish are fed immediately upon arising in the morning, again before departing for work, once at noontime (possibly if someone in the family is home), upon returning from work, and a final feeding before retiring in the evening, the five feedings have been given with minimum inconvenience.

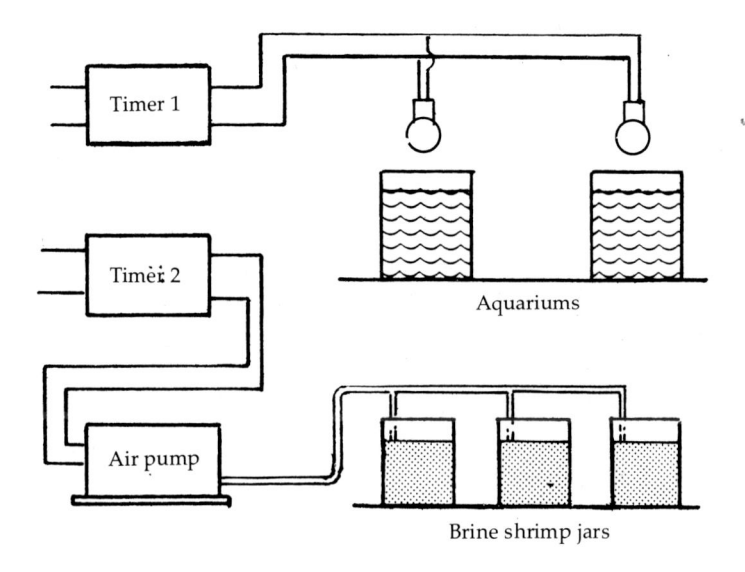

Fig. 5. Two timers — one set to switch on as the other switches off. (See text this page). Wire lamps as shown to ensure that if one lamp fails, the others remain operational.

By employing electric timers to light the aquariums in the morning 15 minutes before one arises, with another timer to stop the airpump which aerates the brine shrimp hatching jars, a first morning feeding need take only several minutes before an early shower. The shrimp can be allowed to resettle during breakfast and another quick feeding is accomplished before departing for work. If this is a heavy feeding, it will nourish the fry well throughout the morning.

A noon feeding can be given by anyone in the family who is home for lunch. This will nourish the rapidly growing fry through the afternoon. A supplemental feeding may be supplied by the first person home in the afternoon. Such family participation in the project is desirable and teamwork should be encouraged.

The second basic requirement for rapid growth is clean water and frequent partial water changes. By replacing some of the water frequently, even crowded fry will continue to grow rapidly. Once the body size of the fry is one-half inch in length, spreading them out among several aquariums becomes necessary. The fry should be less crowded than six fish per gallon for short-finned angelfish and about four per gallon for veiltails. This thinning process prevents fin-nipping among the young angels and ensures superior fin development.

Until the fry are a month old, cleaning by siphoning is usually not required. When very young, siphoning the aquarium can even be dangerous to the fry, since they are often sucked up in the siphon.

At the age of one month, they have grown considerably and the water rapidly becomes foul unless siphoned. It is a common practice to use motor-filters after the fry are one month old. Frequent partial water changes and the use of a motor-filter ensures perfect development for virtually all of the young angelfish.

Partial water changes are also beneficial because they improve the appetites of the young fish, which, consequently eat more and thus grow even faster. This, in turn, ensures even growth among the fry (if they are fed enough). If it is desired to market commercially the fry when they are large enough, consistency in size is of considerable importance in determining the value of the spawn, since professional dealers rarely will purchase a stock of fish unless they are all nearly the same size.

When the fry reach the point where they can be marketed, and the fish breeder is ready to sell, it is advised that he checks with local authorities in his area to determine if any permits or licenses are required for the sale of home-raised tropical fish and examine the later part of this book which deals with small-scale commercial breeding of angelfish.

10. SMALL SCALE BREEDING OF ANGELFISH

Beginning breeders often ask if small scale breeding of angelfish is profitable. The answer is that any business can be profitable, it simply depends upon the person operating the business. Doubtless, a certain business sense is required to run a successful business, but this can be easily acquired through assiduous study and experience.

A breeding aptitude should by now be adequately developed if the reader has carefully studied all of the information presented in this book, as well as others on the subject of general breeding.

With a business sense and a breeding competence, how much money can be made depends upon how much effort the individual aquarist is willing to put into the enterprise. It is entirely possible for a small scale garage operator to raise enough angelfish to gross $1,000 a month, if he is willing to put forth the required effort. This need not seem incredible.

With only seven mated pairs an experienced hobbyist can readily produce 5,000 or more baby angelfish per month at a going average wholesale rate of 20c each. In many cases a knowledgeable breeder can make considerably more than this amount, depending upon his geographic location and the demand for his fish.

Keeping more than seven pairs rapidly thrusts the avocational hobbyist into the status of the professional breeder. Aside from the earning potential of more than seven pairs, the amount of work required to satisfactorily conduct the business rapidly assumes the proportions of a full time job.

Consequently, for the purposes of this book, the author has assumed that the average small scale breeder will have between 5 and 7 pairs of angelfish. Obviously, breeders in certain areas will only have a need for two or three pairs, whereas some ambitious hobbyists may readily conjecture themselves working with a dozen pairs to meet the needs of their large metropolitan area.

Working with a half dozen pairs of angelfish will require a work schedule of about 20 hours per week. This is roughly equivalent to the hours required by any part-time job. The difference is, however, that the hobbyist is doing something he really enjoys at his own home and what he earns is directly related to his own ability rather than determined by company regulations or an indifferent supervisor.

The small breeder will achieve the best results if he restricts his initial efforts to the most popular lower priced varieties. Included as breeding stock in a 7 pair operation should be two pairs of silver angelfish, two pairs of black lace angelfish, one pair of marble angels, and one or two pairs from among the following: black lace veil, marble veil, blush, blush veil, zebra, zebra veil, or half-black. The choice of the last pair(s) will depend upon the demand in each area and the preference of the individual breeder.

The greatest demand is usually for inexpensive silver angelfish. Their low price and hardiness compared to fancy angels makes many breeders hesitate to even bother with silver angels, therefore increasing the demand, lowering the supply, and opening many opportunities for the shrewd beginner.

The inexperienced breeder who thinks he is going to suddenly make a fortune by breeding black veil angelfish, or any other expensive variety, is only fooling himself and his delusion will be costly in terms of time and money. While the intelligent breeder is breeding several thousand angels monthly, and selling them for 15c each, the greedy breeder of fancy angelfish will be lucky to sell 100 of his fish at the inflated price. There is less demand at the high prices and less dealer willingness to take a chance on an independent breeder who is simply out to make a quick dollar.

Black lace and black lace veil angelfish are strongly recommended by the author since these two varieties will produce six types of offspring: silver, silver veil, black lace, black lace veil, black and black veil. This effectively increases the marketable varieties of angelfish without the requirement of extra pairs.

The hardy marble angels have continued to be consistently good sellers since their introduction to the nationwide market in the late 1960's. These should be included in the varieties because they are good sellers, have excellent possibilities for producing potentially profitable mutations, and they are hardy for the beginner.

The remaining fish chosen for breeders will depend upon personal taste and local demand. The most important consideration to the capitalistic breeder will be demand, whereas the hobbyist not really interested in money will cater to his own whims. It does not really matter except that the aesthetically inclined hobbyist had best make provisions for disposing of the hundreds of angelfish that will be raised.

The capacity of the individual's hatchery operation is equally important in determining the production of angelfish. Even though 7 mated pairs of angelfish will have a total egg production approaching 8 or 9 thousand eggs a month, if the hobbyist has only a dozen 30 gallon aquariums at his disposal it is all rather pointless.

As a point of reference, let us assume that 7 mated pairs will each spawn twice monthly, with an average per spawn hatching of about 400 baby angelfish. Thus, as an average figure, let us assume that 7 mated pairs will produce a potential of 5,600 baby angelfish per month.

The population of a metropolitan area which would be necessary for the hobbyist to easily dispose of 5,600 angels monthly, assuming little competition in his area, would be about 500,000 people. Furthermore, these 500,000 people must have a mean income which allows some luxuries in life. Certainly a hobbyist in an area where poverty and starvation are commonplace could not hope to market 5,600 angelfish, unless they were sold to be eaten!

Since the average retailer sells at least 500 angelfish per month, the hobbyist expecting to market over 5,000 angelfish monthly must look for at least 10 outlets. These outlets may include the dime stores and variety outlets as well as the pet shops and aquarium stores.

In order to reach a production of 5,600 angelfish monthly the hobbyist must have an area in his fish room of nearly 400 square feet. The average home basement or two car garage is of about this size and is usually perfectly suited for the raising of tropical fish with a minimum of alteration.

Raising over 5,000 angelfish per month requires a total gallonage of raising space nearing 1,600 gallons. The exact calculation is fifty-one 30 gallon aquariums, or their equivalent, to produce this many angelfish. This is calculated as follows for the entire inventory of young angelfish during a two month raising period.

For the first month, angelfish fry can be crowded at density of nearly 400 fish per 30 gallons of aquarium water. Thus, 400 fry per tank, with 5,600 fry, requires fourteen 30 gallon aquariums for the first month.

During the second month, however, the fry must be sorted and placed in new aquariums which allow for sufficient growth and fin development. A density of 5 per gallon is nearly ideal for normally finned angelfish, while somewhat less density is necessary for the veiltailed strains. Again, by calculating on the monthly production of 5,600 angelfish, and assuming minimal losses, thirty-seven 30 gallon aquariums are required.

Thus it can be seen that fifty-one 30 gallon aquariums are required for a normal production of 5,600 angelfish. While this might at first appear to represent a staggering investment to fully equip a miniature hatchery with 51 plus aquariums, let the reader be reminded that the production output of such an installation will readily pay for itself 4 times over during the first full successful year of operation.

Without going into figures which are rapidly obsolete in our inflationary times, the production of a small hatchery on this scale will produce a potential annual profit roughly equivalent to the earnings of an average lower level management employee. The investment required, providing the price of angelfish keeps pace with the price of equipment necessary to build a hatchery, as I believe it will, is equivalent to one fourth the possible yearly profit.

With these ratios in mind, the hobbyist contemplating the investment of time and money in an angelfish breeding establishment is better prepared to give his decision careful thought. Certainly along with the glowing possibilities, there is also the potential of dismal failure. The author readily admits that everyone is not possessed with the necessary aptitude to make a profit in the breeding of angelfish.

In the author's final analysis, it is entirely possible to make an enviable income, working part time, in the raising and breeding of angelfish. It is, however, something that is impossible to guarantee, since success or failure is entirely dependent upon the individual aquarist.

11. INSTALLATION OF A HATCHERY ROOM

The installation of the hatchery room will require a great deal of forethought. Aside from the previously described necessity of evaluating whether one has the required ability, one must equally consider whether there is suitable space to be had, either at home or elsewhere for a reasonable price.

The initial selection of location for the hatchery room, which should have an area of nearly 400 square feet, or more, must be carefully made. Normally, a two car garage, usable basement, or unused utility room are ideal possibilities. Other rooms prove less satisfactory because of probable water damage and lack of running water or cement flooring.

Basic requirements include suitable insulation and drainage. The insulation cuts heating costs and helps to stabilize temperatures, while drainage provides for easy cleanup with the inevitable spills and leakages.

If a basement location is chosen, care should be taken to protect overhead wooden flooring, since excessive condensation of moisture may cause rotting or warping of exposed wood. It is advisable to first consult an expert as to the likelihood of this possibility; otherwise, eventual damage could rapidly nullify the profits made in several years of work.

Garages offer fewer potential dangers of damage in most cases, but a careful examination of possible problems is indicated.

Alternately, the ambitious hobbyist can sometimes arrange to rent a location for a nominal price when he cannot provide a suitable location of his own. A rented space should have the required cement flooring, insulation, and running water. Heating and drainage are less critical and can be added, but if possible choices exist, those which already possess such advantages should be given priority.

High ceilings must be avoided unless heating will not be required or the landlord offers to install a false ceiling. (A lease will surely be necessary in this instance, however).

Inexpensive rental space may often be obtained from landlords of older buildings who are obliged to lower their rents to attract tenants. Warehouse space or even storefronts are suitable hatchery spaces. A little searching is bound to reveal several such buildings in most neighborhoods.

It is preferable to begin hatchery operations in late spring. This allows at least four months for working out operational problems before the complication of winter heating arises, which will also add to operational expenses. Another advantage is that by winter, when the main selling season arrives, the hobbyist entrepreneur will have his operation in full-scale production, and have a fine stock of angelfish to meet the demands of his dealer friends.

Pre-installation preparation should include raising the breeders and preparing an itemized list of all required equipment. Some items may be acquired in advance by taking advantage of sales, liquidations, and bankruptcies. Equipment may be obtained occasionally at a fraction of its value by an alert hobbyist.

As stated previously, seven breeding pairs is an ideal number for the beginning commercial breeder who is interested in producing an income from his part-time effort. The layout illustrations will be given for a typical hatchery accommodating seven breeding pairs with room for expansion up to 15 or 20 pairs if desired later. Alternately, the hobbyist desiring to begin with two or three pairs may easily utilize all information provided on a smaller scale.

The hobbyist should bear in mind, however, that 20 pairs require three times the tank space as required by seven pairs.

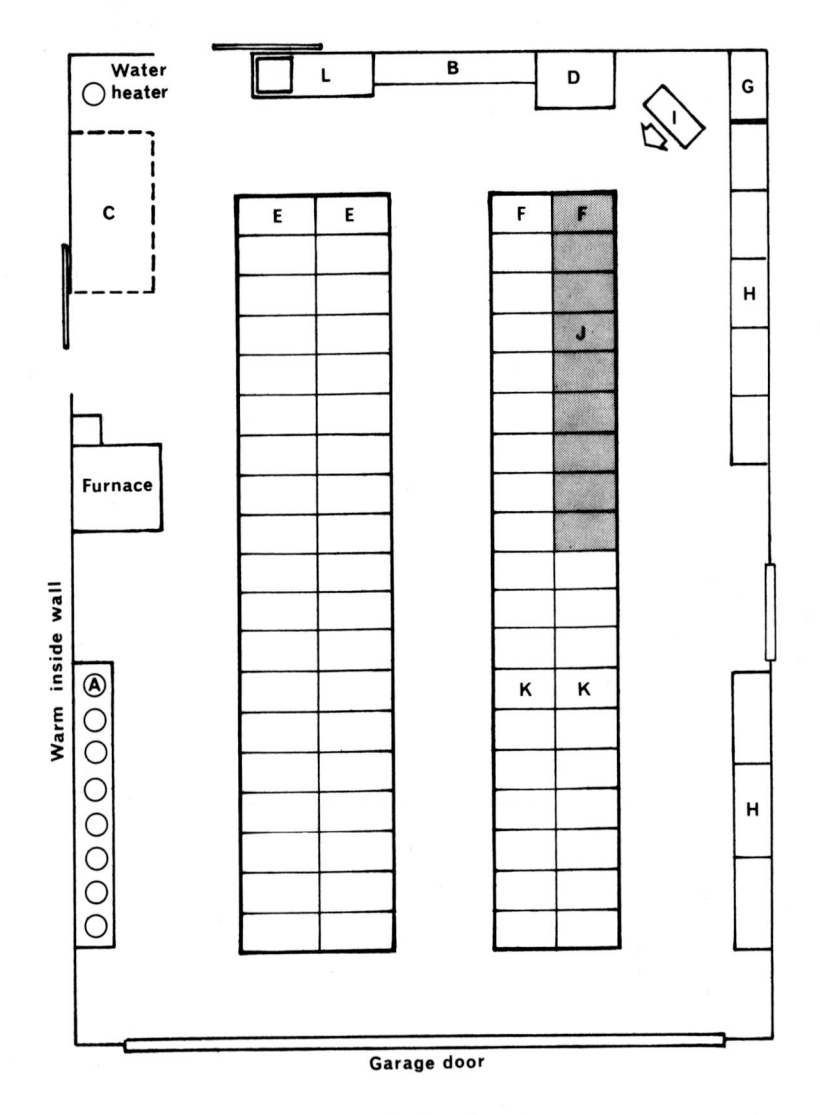

Fig. 6. Hatchery layout.

A. Egg nursery & alevins.
B. Brine shrimp hatchery.
C. Storage area
D. Cold food storage
E. Tank bank
F. Tank bank
G. Pump area
H. Tanks for medium sized fish
I. Heater. Raised.
J. Breeders, top row.
K. Small fry, top row.
L. Work bench.

Basic Hatchery Layout

E: Aquariums, three rows high with aquariums on each level. Two lower levels are with standard 29 gallon aquariums (12" x 30" x 18"), while the upper row has low aquariums (12" x 12" x 30") for smaller fishes. All aquariums side-by-long-side.

F: Aquariums, three rows high with aquariums on each level. Two lower levels are with standard 20 gallon high aquariums (12" x 24" x 16") and the top level can be with either the same or standard 15 gallon aquariums (12" x 12" x 24"). The top row is for breeders (high and warm) and for free-swimming alevins (for the same reason.) All aquariums side-by-long-side.

H: Aquariums for raising medium fish and future breeders and at least one aquarium for pairing off breeders. Three tiers high, placed lengthwise.

This is a typical American two-car garage in the southern United States. Basements, utility rooms, and one-car garages will, of course, be different. This illustrates the basic method of laying out a small home-sized hatchery. However, the hobbyist can devise his own layout to suit his particular situation.

Fig. 7. Typical three-tiered rack for aquariums, showing how they can be nosed in lengthwise to conserve space.

Thus, the hobbyist would need to provide over one hundred and fifty 30-gallon aquariums for the total two month output of 20 pairs.

In a typical hatchery setting, there are several universal requirements common to every hatchery designed for angelfish raising. Space must be supplied for each of the following in almost every instance:

The mated pairs	The eggs and alevins
The fry	Rearing of future breeders
Brine shrimp hatching	Fish food storage
Working space	Air pump
Heater	Water supply and drainage

The afore-listed space requirements are nearly universal in that most every hatchery will require provision for each item. When the aquarist lays out his basic plan for his own hatchery, prior knowledge of each essential requirement will enable him to design his hatchery with a minimum of afterthoughts.

Some basic rules of hatchery layout are listed on page 64 With these guides in mind, an efficient hatchery can be laid out quickly by using the additional information in this chapter. As an example, a typical 20 x 28 foot garage was chosen as an appropriate model. With this carefully diagrammed installation, it takes little imagination for the serious hobbyist to plan his own hatchery within his own available space.

The order in which the installation should progress is given on page 64 Obviously, one should take care of major installation problems before installing the aquariums. It is hoped that this guide will simplify the procedure for anyone wishing to install their own hatchery operation.

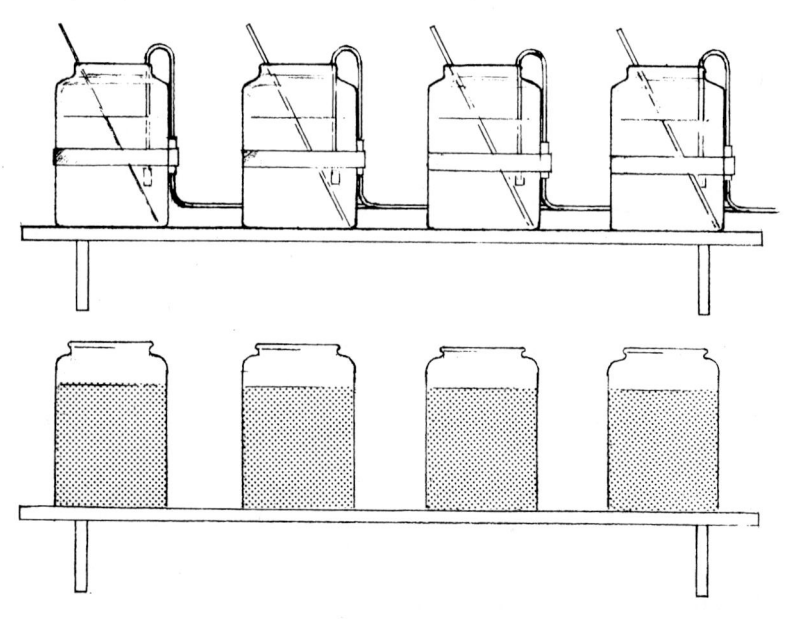

Fig. 8. Incubation jars (top) and brine shrimp containers (bottom). Shelves can be mounted in tiers on wall to make the best use of available space. (Air lines have been omitted from the illustration of the brine shrimp containers for clarity, they should, of course, be installed).

GENERAL RULES FOR HATCHERY LAYOUT

1. Locate angelfish hatching jars, alevins, and brine shrimp hatchery on a warm inside wall away from drafts.
2. Fish food is stored at the coolest, driest location of the hatchery.
3. Working space and brine shrimp hatchery should both be near the water supply and sink.
4. Breeders' aquariums should be situated high to take advantage of warmth and to allow the breeders a panoramic view of the hatchery room.
5. Air pump should be at an outside wall, six feet or more high, yet accessible for maintenance. It should be near an electric outlet.
6. Aisles between aquariums should run away from water source and drainage to simplify siphoning and hose manipulation.
7. Bottom row of aquariums should be a minimum of four inches off the floor to prevent undue coolness.
8. Heater is placed at the point of maximum circulation to efficiently heat the entire room. Auxiliary circulating fans can force warm air downward if necessary.

ORDER OF INSTALLATION

1. Installation of insulation, waterproofing, and preventive measures.
2. Tank layout is chalked out on the floor and room lighting is installed over the future aisles. Any other required electrical work is also done at this time.
3. Aquarium racks are now built and positioned. These are leveled and painted to prepare for the aquariums.
4. Air system is installed above the racks with PVC or similar

piping, and brass pipe valves are inserted. Various techniques are possible; consult the local hardware dealer concerning best joints and bonding material.

5. Shelving is installed for brine shrimp hatchery, work area, and hatchery containers. Locate at about eye level to take advantage of warmer temperatures and to simplify work.
6. Aquariums are installed and leveled, airlines are brought into the aquariums, and filters installed. Aquariums are checked for leaks.
7. Fish are added.

While there is no ideal aquarium size for raising angelfish, in the author's opinion, 29 and 30 gallon aquariums are best suited to the needs of the average aquarist. These provide for the best combination of gallonage, depth (to produce the best fin development, and price.

Twenty gallon low aquariums are ideal for the fry when they are first placed in aquariums, usually for the first month. Being not too deep, the fry can swim and search for their food better than in deep aquariums. These aquariums are also reasonably priced and allow for excellent capacity.

When installing rearing aquariums, it is desirable to locate the shallowest 20 gallon aquariums on the highest rows. This allows the smallest fry to benefit from the most light and the warmest temperatures. Also, by placing the shallowest aquariums on top, the hobbyist is more readily able to siphon and perform other necessary functions without undue inconvenience.

The lighting system should include dim room lighting (probably already existing in most cases) and the previously mentioned aisle lighting. It costs little more to have a 24-hour timer installed on both circuits, and the daily convenience afforded is well worth it.

When the heater for the hatchery is installed, weather stripping should be installed at all doors and windows. With this procedure alone, a savings of up to 25% of the heating bill can be realized.

When purchasing the space heater for the hatchery, which need not be elaborate, it is important to have a thermostat on the unit. Unregulated heating, with attendant fluctuations, is far less dependable and unduly jeopardizes the welfare of the breeding stock and fry.

Aisle space, as shown in the layout illustration, should be at least three feet wide. Any less space between aquariums is impractical and even disheartening as the breeder will be overly cramped when attempting to service his aquariums.

With these guides in mind, the aquarist will be able to design and build his own hatchery with a minimum of inconvenience and confusion. Common sense and a rational consideration of the requirements in each instance will guide the enthusiast in the design of a practical installation.

12. SELLING THE BABY ANGELFISH

Since the successful angelfish breeder not wishing to sell the result of his labors is probably non-existent, it is appropriate to include a chapter on selling angelfish commercially. Writing for those hobbyists unexposed to the workings of the tropical fish industry, the author has tried to explain clearly the manner in which prices are determined for the various sizes and types of angelfish.

If the goal of the hobbyist is profit, and if his product is angelfish, the final requirement necessary to reach his goal is a market in which to sell his angelfish. In some areas, the only outlet available may be a single local retailer, but in most developed areas, there are numerous outlets to sell quality angelfish for a good price. Angels are even in great demand in areas where there are no experienced breeders, and it is in these areas where the neophyte fish breeder is likely to encounter the least resistance to his sales pitch.

Some possible outlets include the many discount and variety stores which deal in tropical fishes. If these retailers buy exclusively from a jobber or wholesaler, then contacting him could result in a single outlet for most of the fish the hobbyist can raise.

Most larger towns have two or more pet shops and a couple of independent aquarium shops which provide the main source of tropical fish for area consumers. These retailers are among the best outlets for experienced hobbyists to sell their tropical fish.

The hobbyist must determine for himself whether he intends

to sell principally to a jobber, at a lower price per fish, but with greatly reduced time and effort expended to market them, or if he intends to market his own fish to each retail outlet at a slightly higher price, but with attendantly higher costs in terms of time and money.

Few experienced breeders hesitate to choose the jobber as a method of marketing their fish, preferring to devote their time to producing better fish rather than chasing after 10 or 15 small accounts. The competent jobber earns his commission by providing a service to both the breeder and the retailers he supplies.

Working with a jobber is certainly wisest since in low population areas a jobber will service several towns and in densely populated areas an experienced jobber can market more fish faster than the individual breeder by grace of his already established marketing pattern.

The prime benefit to the breeder is a saving of time. Since the breeder will probably only be involved with fish on a part-time basis, with spare time consequently at a premium, the saving of time can be directly converted into the production of more saleable fish which in turn compensates for the reduced price paid by the jobber. Thus, the fish breeder can do more of what he likes to do, breeding fish, and leave the selling of them up to a specialist.

Another consideration to the hobbyist turned breeder is that retailers usually prefer to be billed for shipments, whereas the jobber will usually pay for the fish he buys C.O.D. If the breeder should choose to supply the retailers, he will thus be required to have a relatively sophisticated bookkeeping system and invest more time in paperwork than would be required if he dealt only with a jobber.

Once it is decided that the fish will be sold to a jobber, and once he is located, usually by questioning a local dealer, the hobbyist must then approach him with a sample of his fish. Jobbers are notoriously skeptical of novice fish breeders who promise the sky and deliver substantially less. The sample, which should be a free gift, is presented to the jobber so that he can see what you are capable of producing and that you are serious enough to bring him some of your stock.

A second indication of your serious intentions can take the form of a carefully prepared price list. This need only be a typed form, listing the prices which you feel are justified by your quality and experience. Be sure to include the volume prices as well as the 50 and 100 quantity prices. Obviously, if a jobber offers to buy 10,000 common angels, they are going to be substantially cheaper than if he wants to purchase only 50 of them.

The prices to ask for your stock can be readily calculated when it is known that the jobber will pay approximately one-sixth of the current retail price for your fish. This is so because the retailer customarily triples his price and the jobber normally doubles his. Working backwards, a one dollar fish at retail probably costs the dealer about 34 cents. If the fish costs the dealer about 34 cents, then you can calculate that the jobber has paid only about 17 or 18 cents for the same fish.

Why is this so? First, the dealer usually has a very high overhead, high maintenance expenses, and a substantial loss rate to cope with. Thus, in order just to break even he will usually have to double his price. But since he is doing this work presumably to earn a living, something more than just breaking even is desired, thus he must triple his prices. When one considers that it requires the sale of thousands of fish monthly just to meet overhead expenses, this apparently enormous markup is really quite minimal.

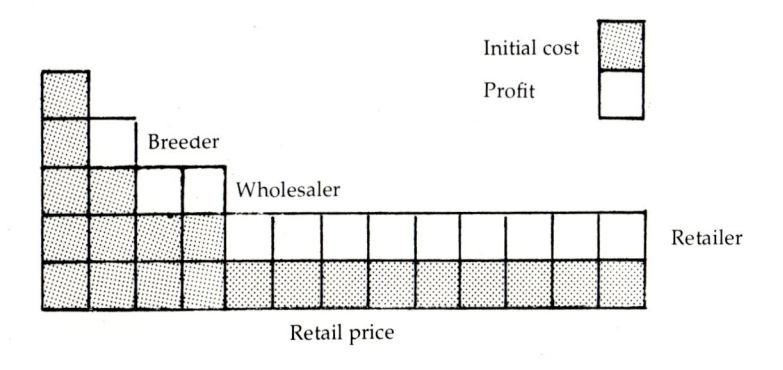

Fig. 9. Diagrammatic illustration of price structure.

The wholesaler has less overhead, sells more volume of fish, keeps them less time, and can therefore mark them up a smaller percentage. Most wholesale jobbers double their prices.

The breeder of angelfish can take advantage of this knowledge and quickly calculate the realistic prices he may ask for his fish. From that point of reference, he may then work with the jobber to determine the exact price that will actually be paid by the jobber.

In order to effectively supply a jobber or retailer, the competent breeder must attempt to determine what the demand will be for the various strains of angelfish. It is, after all, the public which will decide what kind and how many of each fish the breeder should produce.

What the public primarily wants are healthy, full-bodied, colorful, tropical fish that are peaceful community residents. (While angelfish are not always the tranquil beauties they appear, they are nonetheless generally peaceful enough to be included in most community tanks.) The public may have various preferences, but generally they buy fish that look good and are healthy. In general, the difference between blush angelfish and black lace is slight in the public's mind. But when the choice is forced between sick black lace and healthy blush, the consumer is no fool and is going to buy those fish which appear as though they will live longer than the trip home.

When attempting to market his fish, another subtle aid in closing a sale, is for the breeder to have all of his fish the same size. This is the subtle mark of the professional fish breeder, and is a direct result of the amount and quality of care given to the growing fry.

The reason why angelfish must be all the same size for the dealer is not readily apparent to the amateur fish breeder, but is too important not to be considered. Once the reason is explained, the seeming simplicity of the answer leads the novice aquarist one step further toward becoming a seasoned professional fish breeder.

When a busy fish dealer is netting out fish for a customer, it is imperative that all the fish be of equal size. If they are all very similar, the customer is not going to be very picky and will allow the dealer to catch whichever fish is convenient. If, on the other hand, the fish are all of different sizes, colors, and finnage, the consumer is quite likely to become quite demanding in his choice of fish for his home aquarium. With the catching of each fish approximately one extra minute of work will be required to serve the customers. If this is calculated on 100 fish, then there will be 100 extra minutes necessary to sell 100 unevenly matched fish. This amounts to nearly two man-hours of extra labor, and if we calculate the rate at $3.00 an hour, for two hours work, the extra cost per fish amounts to about 6c each.

Thus the dealer is required to pay an extra six cents for fish that are inferior to those he normally receives. It can, therefore, be appreciated why a dealer would refuse a shipment of mixed sized and off-colored fish.

Now that the requirements of the dealer have been examined, let us take a look at how the breeder can determine whether he is making a profit with his fish and what will be the minimum price he can accept. While this may seem a complex computation, it is really quite simple.

In the calculation of his price per fish, the breeder must determine his cost, then double it. It is a simple matter to calculate costs, which include overhead, labor, fish food, depreciation of equipment, and utilities.

Computed on a monthly basis, arriving at the cost is simple. The total costs of production are divided by the number of fish produced, which gives a net cost per fish, and this figure is then doubled. If the operation is run as a business and if a profit is earned, then these figures will be required by the government anyway. If a loss is incurred, it will be in the interest of the hobbyist to keep records also, since then it will usually be tax deductible.

To arrive at the total cost of fish produced, examine one cost at a time. The overhead includes a fair rental value of the premises (if one's own) or the actual price paid to the landlord. Utilities include any water, electric, and sewage bills that may be necessary to pay. If incorporated in the home billing, the just portion attributable to the hatchery should be calculated. Depreciation of equipment may be tentatively calculated at a rate of 1% monthly of the total investment in equipment for the purpose of price determination. Labor is calculated at the rate at which the breeder would be paid were he to spend his time working at a part-time job. Alternately, this figure may be calculated by determining what it would cost to hire someone to do the work performed by the breeder. Fishfood is calculated on the actual amount spent during a month. This includes expenses on brine shrimp eggs and all other expenses for foods. This total should also include expenses such as salt to mix for the brine shrimp water. Finally, any miscellaneous expenditures are added.

While the breeder will readily be able to supply his own figures for any experimental calculations, let us suppose that the total cost of production arrived at by the above explained method would be $500 monthly. If, as intended, the breeder has raised 5,000 angelfish in that month, then it is obvious that the total cost per fish is about 10c each.

Since the breeder has every right to make a profit, just as much right as the jobber and retailer, the breeder must then double his investment and sell his fish for a minimum price of 20c each. If he can sell his fancy varieties at a higher price, so much the better, but he has to average at least 20c per fish to make his operation genuinely profitable.

One must not forget that the breeder is also paying himself a small salary as well. This must be taken into account both when paying taxes and when determining how much profit has been made with the hatchery.

If the breeder wishes to expand his operation and sell medium and adult angelfish as well as the small ones, determining the price of these fish is slightly more complex. The required price is determined by the evaluation of tank space and the length of time it is occupied. If it has been determined, for example, that the average price required to sell a baby angelfish is 20c, then this is the basis for the computation. Since the baby angelfish must occupy tank space for a period of two months anyway, this is the first expense. Since, during any one month period, a 30 gallon aquarium will produce 150 baby angelfish that are readily saleable, then the economic value of that aquarium is $30.00 per month. If the fish which are to be sold as medium fish (only 50 to the tank) require an additional two months in the aquarium before marketing, the total price is two months at $30.00 plus the initial value of the fish (50 at 20c each = $10), thus the cost of the 50 medium angelfish (including expected profit) must be $70, or $1.40 each.

This price is not too high if one is selling directly to the dealer, but if sold to a jobber at this price, the ultimate retail price of $8.40 is out of proportion and very few would be sold.

If the breeder limits his raising of medium fish to those of highest quality of his fanciest stock, then such a price may be justified. Certainly it is wise for the breeder to raise a limited number of medium fish at all times anyway, since there may be an unanticipated demand and the breeder himself may even wish some of the fish for himself for future breeding stock.

The production of mated pairs with the intention of selling them can be a lucrative sideline for the breeder-hobbyist. Since there are always eager initiates of the aquarian hobby willing to spend money for mated pairs, eagerly anticipating the fun and imagining sudden profits, there is no reason the seasoned enthusiast should not satisfy this demand.

Profits from this specialty depend upon the salesmanship ability of the breeder more than anything else, but it is usually a small matter to sell a mated pair for about 30 times the retail price of their offspring. Thus, if a young black lace angelfish sells for 98c retail, it is unlikely that a breeder would sell such a mated pair for less than $30.00. Of course, this is just a guideline price. An eager novice aquarist might be willing to pay even more for a particularly beautiful and fertile pair, while a seasoned fish breeder may abhor paying even so much as $20.00 for the same pair. The price is ultimately determined by the seller's desire and need to part with the pair, and the buyer's desire for and need of the same pair.

If the angelfish breeder desiring to sell mated pairs will approach local aquarium societies, he is certain to find a ready market for some of his pairs, provided he develops a reputation for selling perfect stock with no chicanery. Other possible outlets include dealers' bulletin boards and the local newspaper classified section.

A monthly sales of 10 to 20 extra pairs would certainly be welcome to most breeders and would yield enough to pay the entire overhead expenses of most small hatchery operations.

Selling angelfish, realizing a profit from one's own efforts, and the pride of achievement in producing living beautiful creatures that will give others pleasure, combine to inspire a rare sense of achievement seldom possible in today's urbanized non-agrarian world. In this way, the primal farmer in all of us can be satisfied in a manner that is both highly interesting and profitable.

Appendix A.
SELECTIVE BREEDING OF ANGELFISH

Successful selective breeding of angelfish does not depend entirely upon a solid grounding in genetics. What is more important and certainly more useful is a "wet thumb", nothing more than fish sense, and a willingness to persist with the project through to the end.

If a study of genetics is desired, there are many suitable textbooks currently available explaining the intricacies of heredity, probability of mutations, percentages of offspring which resemble ancestors, and so on. This type of information is of little practical value to the small-scale commercial fish breeder.

A fundamental understanding of some of the basic principles of genetics is of definite value to the small-scale angelfish breeder, however, and the following information attempts to explain a common sense understanding of the elementary principles necessary to selectively breed angelfish.

Selecting top quality young angelfish for breeding stock is an ability which is acquired through experience. A breeder rapidly learns, when dealing daily with thousands of angelfish, to subconsciously evaluate the quality of every young fish. It is really quite easy for any observant person to notice subtle differences among a spawn of young angelfish.

Near perfect angelfish, perhaps 5% of most spawns, have perfect, undistorted ventral feelers, arching backwards and downwards terminating slightly above the lowest part of the anal fin. The dorsal and anal fins must be straight and held erect. Any imperfect fish having fins with kinks, knots, or bends are unsatisfactory as breeding stock. The tail should radiate rays from a symmetrical and strong caudal peduncle and give the impression of an equilateral trapezoid. The uppermost and lowest filaments of the fin should radiate slightly beyond the tail, producing a lyretailed image. No other rays should extend beyond the tail edge. The pectorals should be wide and carried perpendicular to the body and be exactly opposite each other. The gill operculum on each side of the fish should be perfect. It should not be too short, exposing the gill membrane, nor should it be too long making it difficult for the fish to breathe. The body and especially the spine, of the fish should be free of deformity and the lateral line should make a gentle arc across the side of the fish.

Coloration of the specimens selected for breeders should be chosen on the basis of their being representative of their strain. Extremes of coloration should be avoided when choosing potential breeders, since this will lessen the ultimate value of their progeny.

By continually choosing representative stock that is free from deformities, the breeder will be assured of perpetuating a strain of nearly perfect angelfish of which he can be justly proud.

When selecting potential breeding stock to be raised for future matings, never choose exclusively the largest or the smallest fish thinking it possible to produce either a giant or dwarf strain. Since male fish usually grow largest and fastest, while females grow usually slower and remain smaller, the breeder is likely to have either all males or all females for his future breeders.

There is an old axiom, attested to by the earliest fish breeders, many having come from Germany, that breeding stock should never be selected from among the first three spawns of any egg-laying fish, including angelfish. While the reader may dismiss this as mere superstition, it may be founded on some fact as yet unrealized by American breeders. The author personally makes it a practice to select his breeding stock from the fifth spawn of a young pair in the belief that there is nothing to lose by following this old tradition, while there may be much to be gained by the production of superior stock.

A normally productive strain of fancy angelfish will require little improvement after a few generations. Because angelfish produce such enormous numbers of offspring, it requires little effort to select top quality fish from a single spawn. This fact permits the breeder to achieve perfection in a relatively short period of time, something impossible to breeders of mammals, for example, who must work for generations to achieve a similar degree of perfection.

The act of inbreeding — with angelfish it is normally a sibling mating — tends to amplify all predominant characteristics indiscriminately. While the intention may be to enhance a desirable quality, unexpected results may appear just as readily. Maximum effort must therefore be exerted to ensure that fish with undesirable characteristics are not mated, since these characteristics are thus fixed and magnified by inbreeding.

Angelfish should never be inbred more than two generations, since many undesirable mutations begin to occur when the bloodlines have been unmixed for too long. While inbreeding tends to increase the number of mutations, both good and bad, mutations are undesirable for the breeder working on supplying an established market with representative stock.

Outcrossing, mating unrelated males and females of the same strain, tends to add vigor and resistance to disease to a strain. The primary benefit of an outcross, however, is the fact that such a mating normally will minimize undesirable characteristics while strengthening those qualities desired for a representative strain.

Mating unrelated angelfish stock presents a special problem in that all males from one pair must be placed with all females from another strain. This is not easy, since sexing angelfish is tenuous at best. The alternative is to force mate an unrelated pair and then inbreed their offspring allowing free choice of partners. If this pattern is consistently followed, the breeder should encounter few difficulties with deformed fish.

From time to time a breeder may be tempted to try his hand at developing a mutant strain of his own. Aside from the rather lucrative monetary gains possible from a successful venture, most breeders secretly dream of developing their own strain of fish and perhaps having it named in their honor.

To fix a new strain of angelfish requires a great deal of effort, assiduity, considerable luck, and lots of tank space. The basic requirement is, of course, a mutation with which to work. This mutation must be potentially desirable, since nobody would purchase it otherwise. The key fish, or several key fish if the breeder is really lucky, must be carefully reared over the space of one year, given every possible benefit and protection from disease. It should be raised with several of its siblings to allow the eventual choice of a suitable mate from among them.

Meanwhile, the parents also are given the best possible care and all of their subsequent spawns are carefully monitored to discover other possible mutations.

When the fish matures, there are two different courses of action to take. The fish can be mated with its parent of opposite sex, or it can be mated with a brother or sister. Several matings are then produced, and with any luck at all, some similar offspring may appear. If not, some of these young are then raised to maturity for the next step of the procedure.

As the second generation matures, now 18 months later, the mutant is bred to its offspring and some of the offspring are mated to each other. Again the young are carefully inspected and the most representative of the potential strain are selected for future use.

As the second anniversary of the birth of the mutation approaches, he is now bred to the next generation of maturing offspring. By this time, with an ancestry the envy of an Egyptian pharoah, the mutation should begin to appear in sizeable numbers.

If, for example, the mutant was a male, bred to his mother, then to the resulting daughter, grand-daughter-daughter, and great-grand-daughter-daughter, certainly by this time the mutant should be reproduced. If it has not reappeared by this point, it may never reappear. There may have been, as a result of all this inbreeding, newer, even more desirable, mutants that have come along, thus the whole process can be repeated. The chase after new mutants is as elusive as searching for sunken treasure, but it can be a fascinating sideline specialty for the experienced angelfish breeder.

As each enthusiast progresses in the art of fish breeding, he will make new inroads and gain new insight into the working of genetics without spending hours in a laboratory studying fruit-flies or peas, and will probably retain 10 times the knowledge of the subject as his pea-counting contemporary.

Appendix B.
DEVELOPING AN EXPERIMENTAL ATTITUDE

Experimentation can be pursued by anyone, anywhere, at any time. The limits of research through experimentation are bound only by imagination as man continuously seeks hidden answers to his probing questions.

True experimentation requires the preliminary formation of a working hypothesis to endow the experiment with a purpose. This need not appear complicated; it is not. The hypothesis is merely an expressed suspicion which the researcher wishes to either prove or disprove and experimentation is the easiest, quickest, and most reliable method of determining the validity of that suspicion.

If research is to be meaningful, the person controlling the factors must be unbiased and must carefully avoid any preconceived conclusions. Sometimes experimenters subconsciously misinterpret their results to fit their notions of how things should be. It is not always easy to be absolutely objective in examining results which go contrary to one's ingrained prejudices, but if the results are to be meaningful, the experimenter must make every possible effort to remain objective.

Experiments are conducted as scientifically as possible. All known factors are controlled while a single factor or set of factors is varied. Thus, by an orderly manipulation of variables, it is possible to determine the most successful combination producing the most satisfactory results.

While this explanation does not include every phase of experimentation, it is sufficient for experimentation applied to tropical fish keeping and breeding. The goal of experimentation with tropical fish is always an improvement in technique, which in turn produces more tangible results. This is true whether one attempts to improve his private fish food formula or create a new strain of angelfish; it is one's method, or technique, which is subject to continual improvement.

The hobbyist may experiment for a number of reasons. If he is of an inquisitive nature, his primary motivation is probably the desire for knowledge. The resulting benefit for the fishes themselves can be a longer, healthier life. Nearly every hobbyist wants to provide the best care possible for his fishes, but this counts doubly for the fish breeder who earns an income from his fishes as well.

The breeder, through experimentation, can produce larger numbers of higher quality fish with fewer losses and greater disease resistance. This, quite naturally, results in greater profits and deeper satisfaction for the breeder.

It can be readily appreciated by the enthusiast, turned breeder, that he has everything to gain and little to lose by striving, through experimentation, to produce a better strain of fish by improving his methods.

Angelfish breeding experimentation can be divided into three principal fields of inquiry: nutrition, environment, and medication. Undoubtedly, other factors will suggest themselves, but these three points of inquiry are the main concerns of the breeder and are sufficient to begin one's research.

Nutritionally, breeders are always seeking better foods that increase fertility or the number of eggs produced. Simplified, this encompasses the testing of varieties of foods and combinations as well as testing different feeding frequencies. This can include the hobbyist's manufacturing his own foods, perhaps fortified with various vitamins and minerals.

Environmentally, considering just the water for the moment, the chemistry and quality of the water are fluctuating variables which produce multifarious results. The pH and hardness of the water play an important role in the breeding process and careful evaluation of these factors can significantly improve breeding successes.

One seeks to know how the quality, or pollution, of the water affects the fish, the role water quality plays on egg production, or perhaps lifespan.

On the medical front, that is just a term, since it is the hobbyist that often solves many of the enigmas of fish doctoring today, inquiry leads to many interesting challenges. Cures are sought for diseases and side effects are evaluated.

Experimentation, on a small scale conducted by the hobbyist, is what research and development is to the large corporation. By continually striving to improve results, the breeder-hobbyist improves his efficiency and lowers his cost per fish produced, which thus raises the profit realized.

While experimentation is not a prerequisite for success, if the hobbyist is naturally inquisitive he will soon realize that he has what amounts to a hobby within a hobby. By keeping accurate notes on his research, the hobbyist will amass a surprising amount of pertinent information and will rapidly become an authority on many phases of angelfish breeding.

Over the years, the author has found this phase of angelfish breeding by far the most fascinating aspect of the avocation. As long as there are questions that remain unanswered, the hobbyist can find little excuse for boredom with his hobby. It is this fact which keeps the hobby alive and restores waning enthusiasm.

Appendix C.
SEXING ANGELFISH

While there is abundant information available on the subject of sexing angelfish, much of it tends to be frustrating beyond endurance. Some supposedly simple sexual indications border on absurdity in the author's opinion. And other reported indications are apparently either too vague or inappropriate to be truly valid. For example, what good are the positions of angelfish stripes in the sexing of any of the mutant strains? Regretfully they are utterly useless. Because of this, the author has included here his method of sexing angelfish, trusting that it may prove useful to the hobbyist.

This method is far from the final word on angelfish sexing and there are certain to be other published theories showing various methods of sexing these fish, but at least, this method is uncomplicated and anyone who uses it ought to be able to sex angelfish with little trouble.

It should be noted that the fish to be sexed must be mature specimens so that the female has begun to form eggs in her abdomen. Immature specimens have no abdominal bulge like that shown in the illustration on page 00.

Secondly, the fish to be sexed must have been conditioned for about a week on the best foods available and fed as many as six times daily to extend the tubs for sexing. In the side-view illustration shown on page 00 the breeding tubs are shown extended, but it must be remembered that these are usually not visible except at spawning time.

Thirdly, the fish to be sexed should be about the same age, although this is not essential. When a group of angelfish are to be sexed, it is best if they are all from the same spawn, thereby eliminating any slight body differences found in various strains.

The four sexual characteristics that help differentiate male angels from females are: size, breeding tubes, abdominal plumpness, and behavior. Let's examine each separately.

The mature male angelfish is generally about one-sixth larger than the female of the same age. This is not invariably true, but in most cases it is helpful in sexing angelfish.

Next, if the breeding tubes are protruding, it helps in positively sexing. This is easiest to observe when an already mated pair of angels are spawning, but this does not help those hobbyists who wish to force-mate adult angelfish. By feeding mature unpaired fish heavily for about a week, however, the breeding tubs will often extend sufficiently for sexing.

As shown in the accompanying illustrations, mature female angelfish tend to bulge abdominally due to the greater bulk of the egg-producing ovaries. From a head on view, the female's stomach will be noticeably distended, whereas the male's abdomen simply tapers linearly downwards. This bulge is even apparent from the side if the female being examined has eggs.

An additional secondary sexual characteristic of angelfish is seen in the male, who is slightly more aggressive at maturity. This feature is difficult to distinguish at the beginning, but as the hobbyist progresses, it is easier to spot dominant males in an established angelfish aquarium.

Certainly other sexual characteristics exist which may be helpful to the hobbyist who wishes to sex his angelfish, but the foregoing should prove adequate for the needs of most aquarists.

Color Plates

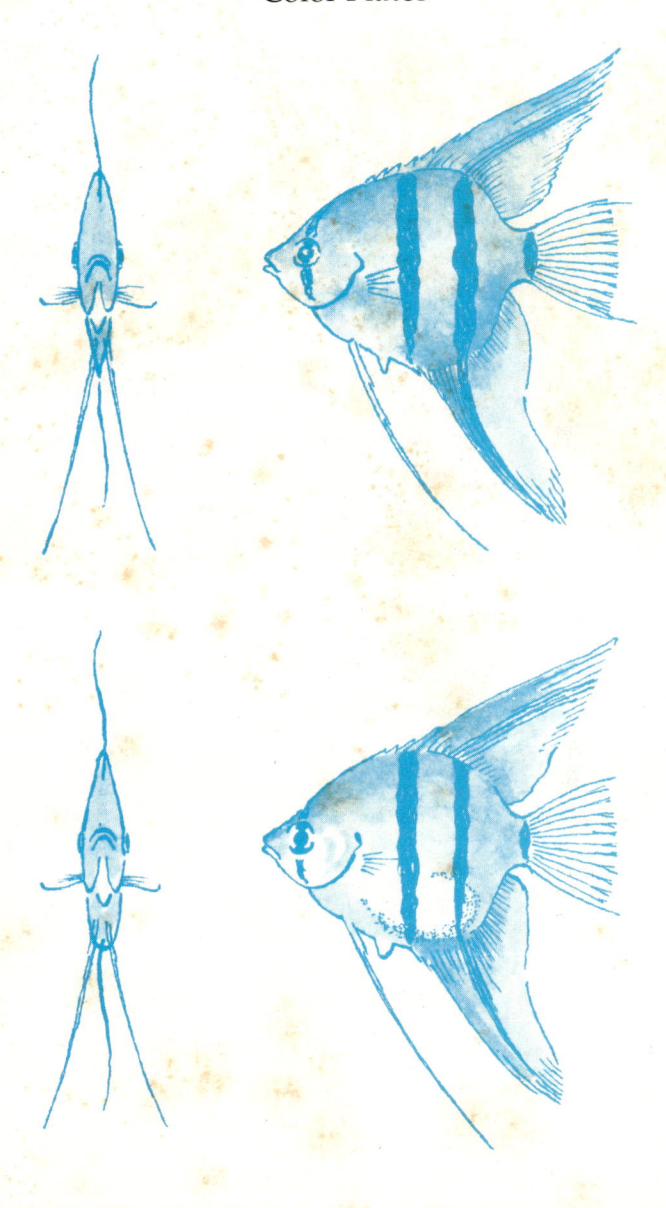

Note the male's breeding tube is pointed whilst the female's is blunt. Male is slightly larger; female with eggs shows abdominal plumpness.

Plate 1. Female Angelfish fanning her eggs.

Plate 2. Female Angelfish about to lay eggs, the male stands by ready to fertilize.

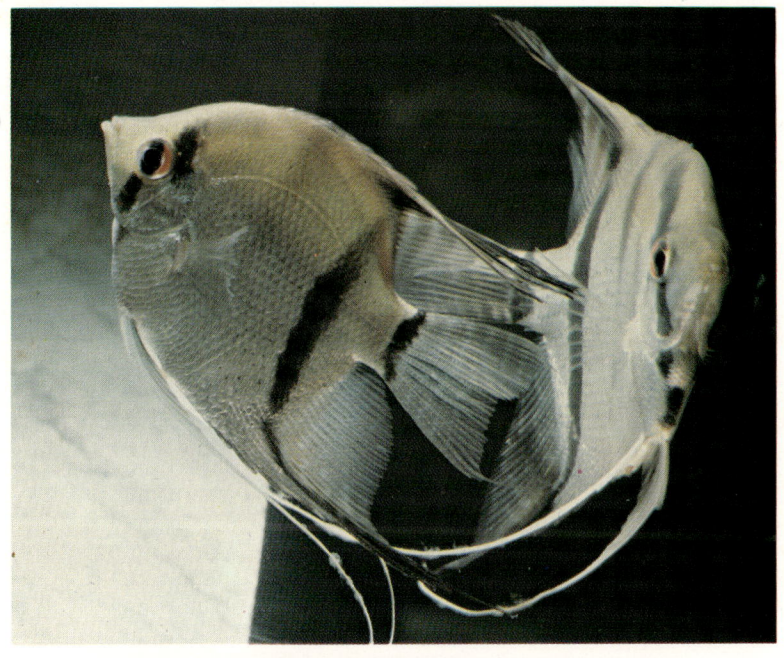

Plate 3. Pair of Angelfish engaged in courtship.

Plate 4. Female ready to spawn. Note the rounded shape of the breeding tube.

Plate 5. Eggs on slate 24 hours after spawning. Note the few white ones that have become fungoused.

Plate 6. Marbeled Angelfish.

Plate 7. Golden Angelfish.

Plate 8. Black Angelfish.

Plate 9. Black Lace Angelfish.

Plate 10. Blush Angelfish.

Plate 11. Silver Angelfish.

Plate 12. Mutant Angelfish with protrusion on head. Not an attractive "sport".

Plate 13. Mutant Angelfish. This specimen is minus its tail, but the fin membrane extends unbroken from the dorsal to anal fin. This fish showed no difficulty in swimming or any other adverse tendencies. The heart-shaped body is not unattractive.

INDEX

Acriflavine, use of	41, 43
Aging of angelfish	24
Airstones	42, 46
Albino angelfish	10
Alevin angelfish	
hatching	37
moving	37
Altering water chemistry	44
Anal fin, angelfish	2
Antibiotics	19
Erythromycin	20
paradox of	20
Tetracycline	22
water soluable	21
Aquariums	
best size for fry	65
cleanliness of	13
heaters for	3
lighting of	12
location of, breeding	36
sizes used	13
stability of temperature	11
timers on	13, 51, 65
Bacteria	13
killing	21
retarding	44
Beef, lean	16
Beef heart	16
Best aquarium size for fry	65
varieties of angelfish to breed	54
Black Lace Angelfish	7, 54
breeding	7
Black Veil Angelfish	7, 54
breeding	7
Blackfinned Blushing Angels	8
Blue Angelfish	10
Blush Angelfish	8, 54
Body form of angelfish	2
Breeding angelfish	25
best varieties	54
choosing stock	76
equipment required	25
history of	5
lazy partner	37
location of aquarium	36
pairing off	25, 27
selective breeding	75
Breeding stock, purchase of	26

Breeding, tubes of angelfish	31
sexing angelfish by	31
sexing angelfish	Appendix C
Brine shrimp	16
eggs for hatching	48
Brown angelfish	10
Buying angelfish	27
Cannibalism, reducing	37
Capacity of production	55
Care of angelfish	11
Care of angelfish eggs	40
Choosing breeding stock	76
Cichlids	
characteristics of	2
intelligence of	2
Classification of angelfish	2
Cochu, Ferdinand	26
Coloration of angelfish	2, 6
Commercial breeding	53
history of	5
Copper sulphate, use of	43
Cost of fish, determination of	71
Cycle, spawning	32
Density per gallon of baby angels	56
Determining price for selling	71
Diet of angelfish	15
relative to spawning frequency	16
Diseases	
finrot	20
mouth fungus	22
prevention of	19, 20, 24
sumptoms of	20
Distribution of angelfish	1
Dorsal fins on angelfish	2
Dosages of medication for	
fish eggs	43
Dry fish foods	16
storage	16
vitamins	16
Duration time of spawnings	32
Egg eating by angelfish	33
causes	35
Eggs, care of	40, 41, 42
fungus of	42
protecting	46
treatment of water for	43
use of acid water	45

Environment of angelfish	13	Habitat of angelfish, natural	1
affecting spawning	34	temperature fluctuation	11
duplicating natural	17	Habits	13
for angelfish eggs	41	Half black angelfish	9
Erythromycin		origin of	9
dosage of	20	Hardness of water	12
use of	20	Harlequin angelfish	9
Experimentation	80	Hatching eggs	46
		Hatching jar for eggs	40
Fanning of eggs by parents	37	Hatchery layout	60-61
Feeding angelfish	15	Heaters	
frequency	16, 17	aquarium	3
natural	17	space	66
for fry	47-48, 50-51	History of breeding	5
Filtration of fry tank	49		
Fin rot	20	*Ichthyophtirius*	20
Fins of angelfish		Incubator jar, use of	40
anal	2	Induced spawnings of angelfish	32
dorsal	2	Intelligence of angelfish	32, 36, 38
rotting of	20		
ventral	2	Jars for angelfish eggs	40, 42
Fish room		Jobbers, selling to	68
heating	12	locating	68
preparation	59		
requirements	58	Layout of hatchery	60, 63
routine	13	Lead, use of	42
traffic	29	Lesions on angelfish	23
Fixing a mutant strain	77	Lighting of aquariums	12
Foods for angelfish	16	stability	12
beef	16	timers	13, 51, 65
beef heart	16	Lion fish, comparison to	10
brine shrimp	16	Live food in diet of angelfish	15
dry food	16	Location of breeding aquarium	36
freeze-dried foors	18		
freshness of	17	Making money with angelfish	53
frozen foods	16	Malachite green, use of	43
list of best foods	18	Markup of price for sale	69
sea foods	16	Mated pairs of angelfish	
Forced pairings	37	buying	27
Freeze-dried foods	18	dominant partner	23
Frozen foods	16	lazy partner	37
Fry of angelfish		moving from tank to tank	37
best tank size for	65	moving their fry	37
feeding of	47-48, 50-51	productive lifespan	24
filtration with	49	sale of	73
numbers of	26		
Fungus eggs	46	Medications	
removal of	46	common use of	21
Fungus, egg	42	for eggs	43
		hard on fish	19
Genetics	77-79	methylene blue	21, 43
Gestures of angelfish, threatening	35	potassium permagenate	21
Ghost angelfish	8	sterilize fish	19
Golden angelfish	8	sulpha drugs	21
Green angelfish	10	use of antibiotics	19

Medium sized angelfish, sale of	73
Methylene blue	21, 41, 43
Microworms	48
Mouth fungus	22
treatment of	23
Moving mated pairs	28
Multifinned angelfish	6, 10
Mutations	
breeding	77
multifinned	6
veiltailed	7
Natural breeding of angelfish	1, 36, 45
pairing off	37
parental protection of eggs	47
Nervous breeders	32
precautions for protecting	32
Netting angelfish pairs	28
Number of angelfish raised	56
Nutrition of angelfish	15
Outlets for selling angelfish	56
Overfeeding of angelfish	17
fry	48
Overproduction of angelfish, preventing	33
Oxygen deficiency	3
in incubator jar	41
Pairing angelfish	25
how to	25, 27
setting up to spawn	29
signs of pairing	28
Parasites on angelfish	22
Parental care	
allowing	34
educational aspect	34
moving fry	37
of eggs	37
retrieving fry	45
washing fry	38
pH	12
Physical characteristics of angels	3
Picking young breeders	76
Postponing spawning	32
Potassium permanganate	21
Preparation of hatchery space	59
Preventing diseases	19, 24
recurrences	22
Price determination	69, 72
Production, capacity of	55
Protecting angelfish eggs	46
Pterois volitans	10

Pterophyllum	4
altum	2, 4, 5
dumerilii	2, 5
eimekei	2, 4, 5
scalare	4, 5
meaning	1
pronunciation	1
proper classification	2
Public demand for angelfish	70
Quinine	
strength dosage	20
use of	20, 22
Rainwater, use of	44
Raising breeders	26
with parents	39
Raising angelfish fry	48-50
Rate of development of fry	47
Ratios of profit possible	57
Red angelfish	10
Removing fungous eggs	46
Renting space for a hatchery	59
Resistance to disease of angels	11
Routine, importance of	35
Schooling tendencies of angelfish	38
Selecting breeding stock	26
Selective breeding	75
Selling angelfish	67
best method	68
licenses	52
mated pairs	73
medium sized angelfish	73
outlets	56
price determination	72
Setting up pairs to spawn	29
Sexing angelfish	31
Sexing angelfish	Appendix C
Silver angelfish	6, 54, 55
Silver, use of	
for egg fungus	22, 43
obtaining	22
preventive for disease	22
Siphoning aquariums	52
Size of angelfish for selling	52, 70
Slate, strips, use of	29, 30, 41
Smokey angelfish	10
Soft water, use of for angelfish	45

Spawning angelfish	30-32	Timers on aquariums	13, 51, 65
cycle	32	Treatment of diseases	22
duration of spawn	32	Tubes of angelfish, breeding	31
postponing	32	Tumors on angelfish	23
precautions during	32		
time of day	33	Varieties of angelfish	6
trial runs of females	31	Veiltail angelfish, description	7
Spawning sites	36	Vitamins for angelfish	
Species of angelfish	4	deficiencies of	16
Sponge filters	49-50	providing	16
Stability of environment			
for angels	11	Washing fry, parental practice	38
importance of	11	Water changes, siphoning	52
Stability of water conditions	12	Water chemistry	12, 81
Starting a hatchery	59	for raising fry	41
Stimulating appetites	17	altering	44
Strain crosses of angelfish	10	Water treatment for	
Stripes on angelfish	2	hatching eggs	43-44
Sulpha drugs, effectiveness of	21	When to start a hatchery	59
Supply and demand of angelfish	70		
Survival of angelfish	3	Young angelfish, sale of	67
		raising	48-50
Temperature requirements	3		
development of fry	48	*Zeus scalaris*	4
maintenance temperature	4	Zebra angelfish	9, 54
tolerance of temperature	3	Zebra veil angelfish	54
Territoriality of angelfish	30, 35		